MR LYAN'S
COCKTAILS
AT HOME

MR LYAN'S COCKTAILS AT HOME

GOOD THINGS TO DRINK WITH FRIENDS

Words and illustrations by Ryan Chetiyawardana

photographs by Kim Lightbody

WHITE LION PUBLISHING

Quarto

This revised edition first published in 2023 by White Lion Publishing
an imprint of The Quarto Group.
One Triptych Place, London, SE1 9SH
United Kingdom
T (0)20 7700 6700
www.Quarto.com

A catalogue record for this book is available from the British Library.

ISBN 978-0-7112-8763-1
EBOOK ISBN 978-0-7112-8909-3

10 9 8 7 6 5 4 3 2 1

Design by Glenn Howard and Sally Bond

Printed in China

This book is dedicated to my sister, Natasha. I can objectively say she's the most talented person on the planet, and can attest that nothing I hold dear would have been possible without her. I love what I do, and I'm eternally grateful for all her hard work in making that happen.

CONTENTS

INTRODUCTION
RYAN CHETIYAWARDANA

We all know a meal made with love can bring people together. Well for me, there's no better route to fun times with friends than serving up good things to drink. This might be down to my own nostalgia – I have great memories attached to enjoying (or making) certain drinks at a specific place or get-together. But when you notice how a well-made cocktail can complement and enhance a social occasion (just as much as food!), it's a huge joy.

I know people are often put off making cocktails because they seem difficult or time-consuming – or that they'll have to stand by the drinks cabinet laboriously mixing complex concoctions while everyone else is having fun. But in reality, making incredible drinks can easily be incorporated into our everyday lives.

Mr Lyan's Cocktails at Home is all about those times when we get together with friends and family, and the cocktails that make those times even more memorable. If you've got a big group to keep entertained, there are batch cocktails that are easy to scale up into bottles, bowls and pitchers. If you're on a chilly winter ramble, opening a flask of something rich and hot will make you even more popular among your companions. Of course, you can chop and change – sometimes a tropical drink on a miserable rainy day can hit the spot so well. But the main thing is, you're having fun – then you'll quickly see how a great drink really cements an occasion.

I've always tried to explore the weird and wonderful through drinks, and incorporate flavours from around the world (this might come from my chef training!). Studying Biology at university led me to understand cocktails on a more scientific level (I've been known to pull all sorts of high-spec equipment and unusual ingredients into play). But those drinks are linked to the amazing teams that bring them to life in my bars. Some involve lots of steps and painstaking preparation, and I rarely find myself going through all that in my house. What I love at home is that crisp martini before dinner, or the refreshing G&T in the garden on a summer evening, or the warming nightcap on a cold evening. These are some of my favourite moments that are made infinitely better by the right drink – and I want to share them in this book.

No cocktail recipe I've included is hard and fast. My hope is that you'll enjoy experimenting with the suggestions. Treat cocktails like you would your cooking. The recipes can be followed exactly or they can simply be an inspiration: adapt them to your own tastes and ingredients. Hopefully all this will mean the drinks you make yourself at home will become more refined. Instead of cracking a bottle of beer or pouring a wine, you'll push beyond your usual calls and try something new. And, hopefully, you'll enjoy your drink that bit more.

DRINKS BY SPIRIT

ALCOHOL	COCKTAIL	
Champagne & Prosecco	Reimagined Bucks Fizz	38
	Bellini	41
	Waggledance punch	74
	Barley Champagne	190
	Spiced Cranberries with Champagne	202
American, Irish & Scotch Whisk(e)y	The Braver	42
	Autumn-Spring Sour	68
	Pass the Buck	76
	Paisley pattern pitcher	81
	Elderflower & Chocolate Scotch with Soda	91
	Manhattan	153
	Smoked Watermelon Shandy	157
	Hunters Flask	162
	Chilled Smoke & Melons	166
	Hot Cold Tea	173
	Het pint	182
	Brewed Brooklyn	201
	Bottled Sweet Martini	205
	Belle Ball	208
Gin	Southside	50
	Rhubarb Leaf	53
	British 45	58
	Garden Buck	64
	Start Me Up Cocktail	67
	Waggledance punch	74
	Grapefruit & Rosemary with Ginger Ale	87
	Diamond Rickey	113
	Mulberry Smash	117
	Gin Basil Fix	129
	Coochin Cooler	138
	Hunters Flask	162
	Fireside Flip	184
	Apple Three Ways	185
	Barley Champagne	190
	Nuked Negroni	195
	Bottled Sweet Martini	205
	House G&T	211
	Tiki G&T	212
	Fancy G&T	213
	Jolly Green Tonic	214
	Tea & G	215
Sherry & Port	Sherry Cobbler	54
	Bubbles & Byass	147
	Barley Champagne	190
	White port & Tonic	217
Rum	Deadly Nightshade	57
	Pineapple Rum with Ginger Beer	93
	Peach & Verbena Smash	118
	Bloody Earnest	130
	Galle House punch	192

ALCOHOL	COCKTAIL	
Bourbon	Harvest Harf	63
	peach & Sage Bourbon	88
	Mint Julep	100
	old Fashioned	150
	Brooklyn	154
Tequila	Rocket to platino	71
	Summer Berry Tequila with Ginger Ale	84
	Death by Julep	103
	Reposado Highball	134
	paloma	148
	Hot Cold Tea	173
Vodka	Golden Cherry Fizz	41
	Rhubarb, pear & Cardamom Vodka with Fresh Lemonade	96
	Gulab Julep	101
	Bottled Cosmo	114
Vermouth	Americano	108
	Vermouth Cocktail	133
	Manhattan	153
	Brooklyn	154
	Barley Champagne	190
	Bottled Sweet Martini	205
	Vermouth & Soda	216
Wine (white)	Bicycletta	111
	Rainy Day Spritz	120
Wine (red)	Golden Cherry Fizz	41
	Chocolate Wine	143
	Smoked Sbiten	160
	Ny Snap	206
Campari	Americano	108
	Bicycletta	111
	Bitter Bubbles	137
	Nuked Negroni	195
Brandy & Cognac	Start Me Up Cocktail	67
	St Clements Cognac with Ginger Beer	94
	Chocolate Wine	143
	Smoked Sbiten	160
	Apple Three Ways	165
	Brandy Blazer	174
	Ny Snap	206
Cider	Hot Buttered Gin	179
Beer	Smoked Watermelon Shandy	157
	Het pint	182
	Brewed Brooklyn	201
Aquavit	Blab Bla Fix	198
Liqueurs	Bumped Hot Chocolate	181

EQUIPMENT

There's plenty of beautiful
(and expensive!) barware out there
(check out some of the stuff from
Japan and Germany), but you really
only need a handful of practical pieces
to make amazing drinks. you'll be
surprised how inventive you can be in
the pursuit of a fine cocktail!

SHAKERS

If you're going to pick up one piece of equipment, I'd say go with an all-metal, two-piece 'tin on tin' shaker for one main reason - they don't break. A distinct advantage when you're making drinks! However, you can adapt when necessity dictates.

Jam jars, bottles and tubs do work, it's just that getting the right amount in - and out - of them is a bit harder.

MIXING GLASS

Again, it's really easy to blow a heap of money here, but all you really want is a medium-sized glass jug. Too small and it won't fit enough ice, too big and the mix churns. Thick glass (or something with a handle) is preferable so your warm mitts don't heat up the drink.

BAR SPOON

A long-handled spoon is a worthwhile purchase, although chopsticks and (clean) paint-brushes also work.

SQUEEZER

Fresh juice is paramount, so a hand squeezer is essential. I opt for the hinged Mexican elbow juice press - it gets all the citrus skin oils out too.

JIGGERS

Stamped measures are required in bars, but at home any consistent measure is fine - a shot glass is ideal. Tablespoons and teaspoons are also useful.

STRAINERS

you'll need to remove the ice and bits from your shaken or stirred drinks. Although a slotted spoon or a sieve will work, a specialist strainer is very useful.

All three will come in handy so are worth having in your kit.

hawthorne   julep   fine

KNIFE & PEELER

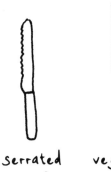  

serrated knife   vegetable knife   y-peeler

you're likely to have these in your kitchen anyway. It's great to have a small plastic chopping board, a sharp paring knife (blunt knives are much more dangerous) and a y-peeler to hand.

A y-peeler is particularly great as it allows you to make strips of citrus zest without catching any of the bitter pith.

GLASSWARE

As with your equipment, it would be easy to spend a small fortune on fancy glassware. A small, quality selection is worthwhile though and will make the final result much better. Each glass shape plays a role in the serve, but as a general rule, go for smaller and finer if possible.

Highball

Named after the family of drinks itself (mixes such as a G&T or scotch & soda), this glass is narrow and thin. It holds carbonation and allows the drink to slowly open out.

Sling

The sling or catalina glass is a relation to the highball. It tapers at the bottom making it more elegant for slings and mojitos.

Shot

A small and sturdy glass for holding around 25ml/1oz. Good as a measure too!

Rocks or old-fashioned or tumbler

These are short and often the heaviest of glasses. This means a boozy nip won't tip over so easily!

Cocktail or California or martini

These should be very small and, ideally, very fine. The drinks served in them are strong so should be cold, short and snappy.

Coupette, sour or daisy

The rounder, larger coupette is brilliant for shaken drinks that have a bit more volume but are served without ice.

Flute

Not only is this nice and elegant, it holds fizz and bubbles well - although a wine glass can often be better to show off aroma.

INGREDIENTS

It almost goes without saying - always use the best ingredients you can. Bad in = bad out. Think about store cupboard essentials, fresh flavours and sparky additions, from sea salt to spice.

Just like in the kitchen, I love to have a few staples to hand that give me a base to make a huge array of drinks with fresh products that I might buy on the day.

Taste every fresh ingredient you're using. you don't need to be able to identify every nuance, but you'll be able to tell if, for example, the oranges from the market are extra sweet, so you'll need less honey to balance.

This will also become important when you start adapting drinks and using your favourite combinations from your cooking. once you get used to the balance of base flavours and tastes - sour, sweet, salty, bitter - you can start to build in accents or modifiers, and substitute your own preferences into the drinks I've presented.

keeping several bottles of different spirits makes sense if you mix
a lot of cocktails at home, but filter down to those you drink regularly.
Although they won't go off, they taste better fresh.

Some ingredients are stable, others want to be kept cool, or used quickly...

Stable

Angostura   Campari   Absinthe (+   triple sec +
bitters   dropper bottle)   fruit liqueur

Cold/fresh

Sugar Syrup

dry + sweet
vermouths

fino
sherry

small, good-quality tonic, soda,
ginger ale/beer

jam

Dry

Sea salt

good quality
local honey

loose-leaf tea

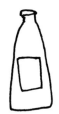

raw cider vinegar

dried spices

maple/kitthul
syrup

GARNISHES

In many ways, garnishing can seem superfluous or an unnecessary step to take, but done right it can be an amazing visual or aromatic addition. Sometimes garnishes complement the serve, other times they contrast. Think about where they're positioned in relation to these two effects - for example, a nice bit of mint next to a straw immediately suggests freshness.

Citrus

Wedges are easier to squeeze than slices or wheels.

Take long lengths of citrus peel using a y-peeler.

Herbs

Give herbs a little 'spank' to release the oils and aroma before you place in or on the glass. Don't tear or bruise them to avoid 'off' or bitter flavours.

you're going to use lots (lots!) of ice, so keep a drawer in your freezer free (what else do you need in there aside from ice cream?). Freeze large cubes from a tray and even bigger-format ice in moulds or trays/tubs.

Ice is one of the most essential components of the balance of your drink, providing aeration (in shaking), dilution and chilling, so don't be tempted to overlook it.

you can also scissor-snip out the dividers in silicon ice trays to make larger ice that fits your glassware.

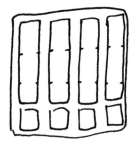 

TECHNIQUES

you'll find a comfortable method quickly enough, but some basic pointers will help you shake, stir and strain with ease.

SHAKING

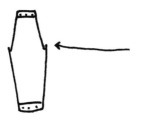

Get used to putting your shaker together - it should form a good seal. Hit the join with your palm and the seal should break. Just hold it tight and don't overfill!

Add your ingredients to the smaller tin without ice. Start with the cheapest ingredient in case you mess up. If you're using anything thick - like honey or jam - stir it in to dissolve before you shake.

Fill the small tin (with your ingredients) with ice (to the top!) then tap the second tin on top.

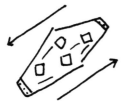

Put your weaker hand on the larger tin and your dominant hand on the smaller. Holding tight, vigorously move the tins back and forth getting as big and quick movements as possible. It should take about 15 seconds, but you'll get used to that.

STIRRING

It's a good idea to keep your mixing glass chilled or frozen if possible, but just make sure it's not warm.

Add your ingredients to a jug and stir to mix.

Fill the jug with ice - as much as you can fit, but not so it's spilling out.

Gently but briskly move the spoon around the inside of the jug. It should hug the glass while moving the ice and liquid in a smooth motion - you don't want to churn or aerate the mix.

STRAINING

Once you've shaken or stirred your drink, you need to remove the spent ice and fragments to serve. If you've shaken the drink or if it has lots of small bits, the best way is to 'double strain' it.

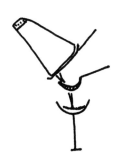

This involves using a hawthorne strainer held tightly to the tin, and a tea or fine strainer between the flowing liquid and your glass.

It's a simple step, but a key one in keeping the drink balanced. Pour quickly and with confidence!

MUDDLING

Most soft herbs and berries don't need breaking apart, as shaking or stirring will release their flavours without drawing out bitter notes.

However, some hardier fruits (such as pineapple) benefit from a gentle crushing (muddling) with the end of a small rolling pin. This technique also works if you actually want a touch of that bitterness too.

BUILDING

Building seems simple as it involves assembling the drink in its serving vessel, but take care to ensure the balance and structure of the drink are maintained, particularly if you've got a fizzy element in there.

Fill your glass (chilled if possible) with ice.

Add the main ingredients, stir, then fill with more ice.

Top off the serve (with fizz) and give a quick stir.

Add a straw and garnish.

SYRUPS AND BITTERS

Making your own sugar syrup
is super-easy - and adding fresh
ingredients you love will create
a bespoke syrup you can't buy
in the shops. Bitters are slightly
harder to master, but even more
rewarding when you do.

HOMEMADE SYRUPS

Sugar and alcohol are great at carrying flavour. They're also effective preservatives so can help you enjoy those lovely fruits and spices that are no longer available in shops (much better than buying those out-of-season strawberries that taste like potato).

To make a simple syrup, start by heating 1 part water until boiling.

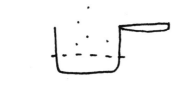

then remove from the heat and add 2 parts sugar.

stir until all the sugar is dissolved. That's it!

To create a unique flavoured syrup, you can easily infuse it with spices, citrus peel or fruit. Just add your choice of ingredient to the hot syrup and stir. Allow to cool, then strain. you can bottle the syrup and keep for 2-3 weeks in the fridge.

HOMEMADE BITTERS

There's a variety of bitters on the market now, but making your own is great fun. I describe them as 'seasoning', or the salt and pepper of cocktails (I even made a salt and pepper bitters once!). They bridge flavours and help give length and depth to a drink.

To make them, you need a bittering agent (like root, bark, leaf or peel), some high-proof alcohol (or vodka if you have nothing else, but the higher the ABV the better), and a range of flavour agents such as herbs, spices, flowers or even nuts.

It's best to steep each bittering and flavouring agent individually in a very small amount of high-proof alcohol (play around with dry-toasting them first). Then you can blend the steeped alcohols together to make your bitters.

Steeping times vary from a day to a couple of weeks. To check it's ready add a few drops into a glass of water to determine whether you can taste the flavours.

Good base-bittering agents

gentian   wormwood   quassia

These are super-bitter, so you don't need to use a lot

Good flavour-modifying agents

orange peel   ginger   clove   cinnamon coffee

you can use more of these spices and herbs

More gentle-accent flavour agents

lavender   dried cherry   juniper   star anise

Try adding burnt sugar for a little richness and depth

Final step

once your different brews have steeped, blend them together, strain through a sieve, bottle and rest.

A proper cocktail has an amazing ability to make a gathering with friends even more magical. These are some of my favourite drinks to make for a host of different occasions...

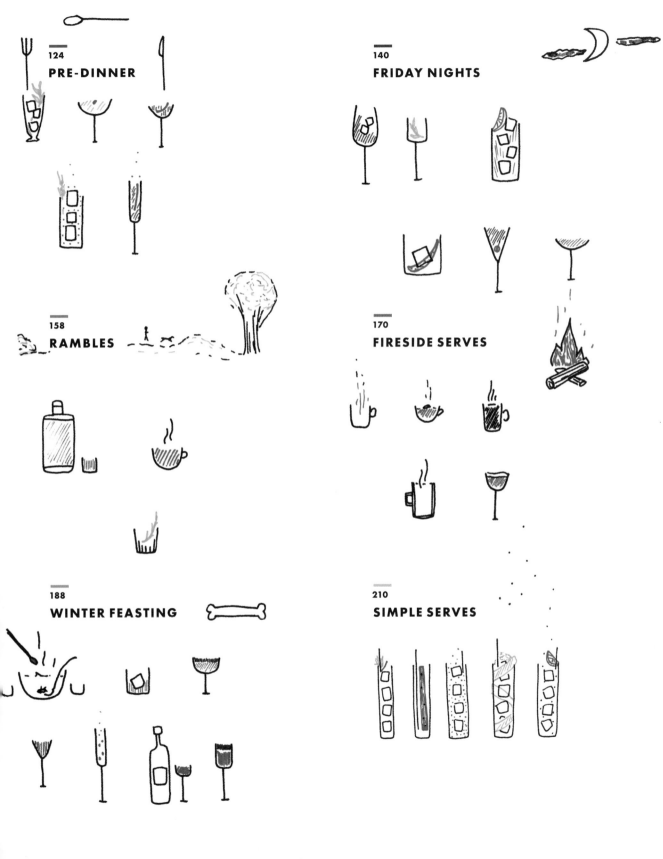

124
PRE-DINNER

140
FRIDAY NIGHTS

158
RAMBLES

170
FIRESIDE SERVES

188
WINTER FEASTING

210
SIMPLE SERVES

MORNING BUZZ

Brunch is one of my favourite times
to have a lazy catch-up with friends.
These light, bright cocktails reflect
the laidback mood (they're not too
full-on!), and can turn a morning into
a celebration rather than a chore.

REIMAGINED BUCK'S FIZZ

Gather

4 tangerines
(or clementines or mandarins)

1 sweet juicing orange

½ lemon

1 bottle chilled champagne

Flutes or small coupette glasses

This is everything you want from a morning cocktail – a bit of kitsch fun, easy to pull together for a group of people, and radiant and uplifting with a splash of fizz. This drink blends three different citrus juices: they boost the bubbles and bready notes of the champagne and stay fresh. I've used tangerines, but clementines, mandarins or any of the more perfumed types are terrific too. The key is balance, so it's not too aromatic and sweet, but similarly, not a fizzy glass of orangey acid. I love the sharpness from lemons beside the sweet plumpness of juicing oranges – the ones that look a little gnarly, but provide the best flavour.

Method

Halve the tangerines and quarter the orange, if necessary, saving some of the tangerine peel. Squeeze through a tea strainer into a small jug, making sure the juices are mixed.

Add just over a shot (30ml/1.2oz) of the mixed juice to each glass and top with champagne (add the champagne in two stages so it doesn't fizz over). Twist a piece of the tangerine peel over the top (to release the oils) but don't drop it in.

Magic

For extra zestiness, save the peels and twist them skin-side down above the jug to coax the oils out (you should notice them appearing on the surface of the juice). Mix well, and the oils will give the whole thing a sherbety tang.

BELLINI

Gather

2 white peaches

6 shots (150ml/6oz) moscato wine

1 tablespoon acacia honey
(if required)

1 bottle chilled prosecco

Champagne flutes

This fizzy number is all about summer decadence. It's perfect with white peaches (or 'doughnut peaches') when they're in season. Failing that, the tinned sort work a treat too, but tend to be a bit on the sweet side without the fragrant bite of the fresh ones. I like to keep the Bellini rustic and simply blitz up the fruit, but strain the purée if you want something smoother. You can also add bright herbs and spices (thyme or cinnamon will both join in happily here), although when peaches are at their seasonal peak it doesn't need much else. If the fruits are a little tart, I like to use some acacia honey for perfect balance – it's clean and floral.

Method

Remove the flesh from the peaches and add to a blender or food processor with the moscato. Blitz on high power until the mixture is smooth. It should flow – if it's too thick add a splash of water. Taste, and if it's on the tart or dry side, add a touch of honey and blend again. Go easy… you can always add more.

Add 2 shots (50ml/2oz) of purée to a small jug and then around 4 shots (100ml/4oz) of prosecco (don't use a measure though, it will flatten the bubbles). Gently churn, lifting the purée through the prosecco, being careful not to knock the bubbles out, and pour into a chilled flute. Add a splash more prosecco if needed. If you have a big jug you can make three at a time, but do it quickly: the gentle fizz is essential to the summer feel.

Magic

Once you get the hang of the balance and the process of making this, you can try different fruits. Apples, pears or sweet plums make a great Bellini (use a touch of lemon juice to brighten), and even nuts such as almond and chestnut can be paired with stone fruits in a purée (although you'll need to cook and strain them first).

THE BRAVER

Gather

1½ shots (40ml/1.5oz) blended scotch (light, although something bolder with a hint of smoke makes a brilliantly deeper version)

2 teaspoons Cointreau

1 tablespoon lemon juice

2 teaspoons lime juice

1 tablespoon sugar syrup (see p31)

3 mint leaves

4 dashes absinthe

1 dash Angostura bitters

Small highball

Cubed ice

Chilled soda, to finish

Lemon, to garnish

Although this might sound full-on for brunch (especially if you're hungover), trust me: as a pick-me-up The Braver punts a Bloody Mary firmly out of the park. It's similar to the scotch classic Morning Glory Fizz, and it's bright and pleasingly complex. There are a fair few ingredients in the mix, and shaking drinks for a group might be the last thing you feel like doing in the morning, but it's worth it. It's also a great example of the magic of absinthe in cocktails. Don't be put off: absinthe lifts drinks in a wonderfully stimulating and 'green' way. A good tip is to buy a small bottle of absinthe and decant it into a dropper or spray bottle (a little goes a long way).

Method

Using a peeler, remove a long 'horse's neck' (a full strip from round the whole fruit) of lemon peel and set aside.

Add everything else to a shaker (except the soda) and shake hard with ice. Double strain over fresh cubed ice into a small highball glass (see p27). Top with soda and garnish with the long piece of lemon peel. Drink immediately and enjoy the revitalising effects!

Magic

There are a lot of ingredients in this drink, each subtly making the whole all the more interesting, but you can add more provided you do so with care.

I often use the straightforward likes of soft berries (particularly raspberries) or herbs (coriander or tarragon) that I might have in the kitchen. But a small spoonful of jam, a couple of cloves or even some green tea leaves shaken through the mix will fit right in.

MARKET FRESH

Farmers' markets are amazing places to go for inspiration – they've given us access to better, fresher and more seasonal ingredients. I love wandering around with friends, chatting to producers and deciding what to cook... and what drinks to make too.

GOLDEN CHERRY FIZZ

Handful of fresh cherries

10 shots (250ml/10oz) light red wine

1 tablespoon golden caster sugar

1 teaspoon loose-leaf Earl Grey tea

4 shots (100ml/4oz)
Regan's orange bitters

Just over a shot (30ml/1.2oz) vodka

Just under a shot (20ml/0.8oz)
lemon juice

1 egg yolk

1 tablespoon sugar syrup (see p31)

Chilled small, narrow highball

Cubed ice

Chilled soda, to finish

Coin of lemon, to garnish

Fresh cherry, to garnish

Fresh cherries are one of my favourite fruits. When in season they can run the gamut of floral and bright, right through to something very deep and autumnal. This drink works with both, but the combination of the deep purple of a black cherry with the wine and the richness of the yolk is particularly special. Speaking of, the yolk might seem odd (and you can omit it if you're serving it vegan style, but also check your wine if so!), but it gives a wonderful richness to the drink in the style of the classic Golden Fizz so is well worth trying. Keep the fruit after the infusion, too – they are great folded into salads, or served alongside cold cuts.

Method

Add the tea to the orange bitters, leave to infuse in the fridge for 24 hours, then strain.

De-stone the cherries, slice, then add to the red wine and sugar in a microwave-safe container. Stir, cover, then blast on high in the microwave for 5 minutes. Allow to cool, then strain.

Add a shot (25ml/1oz) of the cherry wine mixture with the vodka, lemon juice, egg yolk, sugar syrup and 4 dashes of the infused bitters to a shaker. Shake without ice, then add cubed ice and shake again. Double strain into the chilled highball without ice (see p27), then crown with soda. Snap the lemon coin over the top, then discard. Garnish with a sliced cherry placed on the rim.

Magic

You can switch up the wine depending on the fruits you can get, but think about the drink as a whole. The Earl Grey bitters work great with the cherries and the wine, but try to use a tea flavoured with real bergamot if possible (I love Rare Tea Company's Earl Grey for this reason, and for the quality of the tea), but you can also vary the tea accent depending on your fruit. Lastly, use a true vodka that has character rather than sugar as a profile – grain vodkas work brilliantly here, so look for a Polish vodka, or one of the great smaller, local brands that have cropped up.

SOUTHSIDE

Gather

1 small cucumber

8-10 mint leaves

1 shot (25ml/1oz) lime juice

1 tablespoon sugar syrup (see p31)

Splash elderflower cordial or cloudy apple juice (optional)

2 shots (50ml/2oz) gin

Sling or other tall, narrow glass

Cubed ice

Chilled soda, to finish

Mint sprig, to garnish

Mint and small, thin-skinned cucumbers from markets taste far superior to supermarket varieties – and when elderflower blossoms are swamping the country, look for its fresh cordial. You often find amazing heritage apple juices too – again, leagues better than store-bought versions.

All these ingredients combine in this more vivid cousin of the Mojito. It's exactly the kind of drink you need when the sun makes its summer return and you want something uplifting to take out to the garden. It's served over cracked ice, so dilutes pretty quickly; this is great as the drink changes character as you sip, but prepare each glass in the moment to avoid watery slush.

You can buy crushed ice, but a tea towel and rolling pin do a stand-up job. Take a clean tea towel and put ice in the middle. Fold over and give it a few choice whacks. Don't smash it to powder, you just want to crack the ice.

Method

Using a peeler make a long slice of cucumber lengthways (discard the first couple of strips of skin), and wrap it round the inside of the glass.

Add the other ingredients to the glass, then the cracked ice, and gently stir. You just want to churn the mint – if you tear or pound it, it'll taste bitter. Fill with more ice, then crown with soda. Add a straw and put a big sprig of mint beside it (give it a slap to get the aromas going).

Magic

When blackberries start to appear on hedgerows, pick a few and fold them through the mix. They turn the drink a luminous purple, and give a great richness.

RHUBARB LEAF

Gather

2 sticks rhubarb

500g/20oz sugar

300ml/12oz water

2 shots (50ml/2oz) gin

1 shot (25ml/1oz) lemon juice

2 raspberries

1 egg white

Chilled coupette glass

Cubed ice

Granulated sugar, to garnish

Whenever rhubarb's red stems start to appear at the market, I can't help but think about making this drink. There are a few good rhubarb cordials available to buy now, but I'd suggest making your own. Once you taste this cocktail you'll happily go through the whole batch.

This is one of those fruity yet vibrant drinks that everyone seems to love. The egg white creates a soft cloud of flavour, not too sweet or too sharp. You won't taste it, but its texture is paramount as it holds the taste on your tongue. Use freshly cracked organic eggs from your buddies at the market. You can make rhubarb ice cream with the leftover yolk, some cream/milk and the syrup.

Method

To make a rhubarb syrup, slice 1 stick of rhubarb and place in a pot with the sugar and water. Bring to a rolling boil. Remove from the heat, cool, then strain.

Add just under 1 shot (20ml/0.8oz) of the syrup to a shaker along with the gin, lemon, raspberries and egg white. Shake first without ice, then with ice. Double strain into the glass (see p27). Cut a strip of rhubarb, dip in sugar, and lay across the surface.

Magic

You can also blitz the rhubarb syrup before straining it. This yields a more concentrated syrup – almost like a purée – which gives the drink a thicker texture and even more of that trademark tartness.

SHERRY COBBLER

Gather

1 wedge orange

1 cube pineapple flesh (no skin)

1 wedge lemon

3 shots (75ml/3oz) fino sherry

Splash sugar syrup (see p31)

Wine glass

Cubed ice

Chilled sparkling wine, to finish

Berries, to garnish

Mint sprig, to garnish

Icing sugar, to garnish

I love sherry. From the amazing aperitif of a crisp, bone-dry fino to the nutty notes of a well-aged amontillado or oloroso, it's one of my favourite drinks. And it also makes incredible cocktails. My good friend Bob and I have sipped our way through numerous iterations to find the ideal combination. And with my bar buddy Iain Griffiths I also tested tonnes of cocktails while planning a sherry event. But even after all that extensive 'research', the Cobbler remains a firm favourite. Sherry plays well with many fruits too, jumping from citrus to tropical with incredible ease. Don't throw in too many at once, but two or three different types from the market will come together nicely.

Method

Add the ice to a clean, dry tea towel, fold over and give a few whacks with a rolling pin – just to crack it.

Add the orange, pineapple and lemon to a shaker and gently press with the end of a rolling pin – you want to draw out the flavours from the citrus skin too. Add the sherry and the sugar and some cracked ice.

Give it a short shake – a couple of turns up and down – and then strain into a wine glass. Top with more cracked ice and add a splash of fizz. Give it a quick stir, then ornament with berries and herbs from the market and a dusting of icing sugar.

Magic

Sherry has a huge range of flavours depending on how it's processed – 'biologically' under yeast produces greener, dry fino style, and 'oxidatively' creates the raisiny, nutty oloroso style.

Match your fruit depending on the bottle you have to hand and check for sweetness levels. Citrus can jar with some of the darker styles of sherry, but these take to berries and tropical fruit like a treat.

DEADLY NIGHTSHADE

Gather

2 medium aubergines/eggplants

240g/9.6oz demerara sugar

8 shots (200ml/8oz) water

Pinch sea salt

1½ shots (40ml/1.5oz)
golden rum

Just under 1 shot (20ml/0.8oz)
Lillet Blanc

1 shot (25ml/1oz) lemon juice

1 tablespoon demerara sugar syrup
or honey water (see p31)

1 shot (25ml/1oz) egg white

Chilled coupette

Cubed ice

Autumn nights demand opulent and satisfying drinks to stand up to the weather, but when it's not quite winter, a little brightness is welcome too. This rum sour is ideal. Golden and sweet, it has a savoury, vegetal note (literally) that seems tailor-made for when the low sun is out, the leaves have turned and a chill is beginning to set in. It's also really fun as it uses an ingredient not usually found in cocktails, but one that finds itself at home here. Plus the eggplant chips (I've spent too much time working in the States of late; the lingo is rubbing off on me) are the most addictive garnish ever.

Method

To make the purée, split one of the aubergines lengthways. Sprinkle the cut side with 20g/0.8oz of sugar and roast in a medium oven for 20 minutes or until soft and lightly golden. Blitz until smooth in a blender with 200g/8oz of sugar and the water. When smooth, pass through a sieve and reserve (it'll keep in the fridge for 3 days).

Halve the other aubergine lengthways and thinly slice. Sprinkle with the rest of the sugar and the salt and bake in a low oven for 40 minutes, turning once. They'll go crisp and golden – the thinner ones might curl and burn a little, but they'll still taste awesome.

Add the rum, Lillet Blanc, lemon, sugar syrup, egg white and 1 shot (25ml/1oz) of aubergine purée to a shaker and shake hard without ice. Fill with ice and shake again. Double strain into a glass (see p27), and garnish with aubergine crisps.

Magic

Aubergine in a cocktail? Why not! Lots of vegetables take on an intense sweetness when cooked, roasted or dried, so play around with some of the more esoteric ones – as long as it's edible it can be made into a drink. I once created a similar drink with roasted cauliflower and a touch of chocolate, and it was delicious.

BRITISH 45

Gather

3 sticks celery

1 raspberry

1½ shots (40ml/1.5oz)
Mr Lyan Diamond Rickey

Chilled flute

Cubed ice

Chilled champagne, to finish

I've been working with Iain Griffiths (aka The Dude) for a few years now and we've become great collaborators (as well as him becoming very much family). He's been integral to many of the projects I've been involved in, and we've created so many drinks together, but I sometimes miss just being able to visit him in a bar and ask him to make me something tasty. So I was really thankful for this gem he once presented me with on a morning get-together. It's everything you'd want from a revitaliser and is a joyful celebration of British produce at its best. My Mr Lyan Diamond Rickey adds an amazing complexity to this cocktail with minimal effort: all you have to do is open the bottle!

Method

Juice the celery in a juicer. Add to a shaker the raspberry, Mr Lyan Diamond Rickey and 1 tablespoon of the celery juice. Shake with ice, double strain into the flute (see p27), then top with champagne.

Magic

Mr Lyan Diamond Rickey is a blend of my own gin with falernum (a spiced almond and lime liqueur), a little sugar and acidity, and distilled fresh grapefruit and lime.

If you haven't got a bottle to hand, use a shot of gin (25ml/1oz), a tablespoon of lime juice and a splash of sugar syrup (see p31) or falernum.

HARVEST HARF

Gather

½ lemon

2 apples

3 tea bags

250g/10oz sugar

250ml/10oz water

2 shots (50ml/2oz) bourbon

Highball

Cubed ice

Chilled soda, to finish

Mixed market berries, to garnish

Robin Honhold was the manager of my former London bar White Lyan, and his eye for detail is incredible (he's a trained mathematician!). Like me, he's an alumnus of legendary Edinburgh cocktail bar Bramble, and his understanding of the structure of drinks is second to none – as demonstrated by his Harvest Harf. Robin's cocktail embraces the idea of market-fresh produce perfectly, here using berries and local apple varieties to great effect, but with a formula that would work with most fruits. The tannins from the tea also ensure it isn't too sweet and has lingering length.

Method

To make a tea syrup, slice the lemon and the apples, putting aside a slice of apple per serving for garnish. Add to a pan with the tea bags, sugar and water. Bring to the boil, gently mash, then remove from the heat. Allow to cool then strain into a small jug or bottle.

Fill a highball with ice, then add 2 shots (50ml/2oz) of bourbon and 2 shots (50ml/2oz) of the tea syrup. Stir, top with more ice, then fill with soda. Garnish with berries and sliced apple – or any market fruit you've used in the syrup.

Magic

This is a recipe that works hot too. You can vary the fruit according to market availability and then use a formula of 1 part syrup, 1 part bourbon and 3 parts hot water in lieu of the soda – use a pre-warmed mug (and obviously skip the ice!).

GARDEN BUCK

Gather

Handful fresh sugarsnap peas

4 shots (100ml/4oz) water

100g/4oz sugar

1 stem asparagus

2 shots (50ml/2oz) gin

Just under 1 shot (20ml/0.8oz) lemon juice

Small highball

Cubed ice

Chilled ginger ale, to finish

English gardens have such an evocative smell about them, and the flavours that really sum this up for me are peas, mint and asparagus. These aren't ingredients you'd usually expect to find their way into a drink, but two of them form an amazing vegetal backbone to this gin buck ('buck' is an old name for a cocktail involving ginger ale and citrus).

Method

To make pea syrup, place the peas, water and sugar in a small pan and bring to a rolling boil. Remove from heat, allow to cool, then blitz and strain.

If the asparagus is really fresh, peel long strips starting at the base, otherwise cut lengths with a knife.

Fill the glass with ice then add the gin and lemon. Add 2 teaspoons of pea syrup and two strips of asparagus. Stir. Add more ice, then top with ginger ale.

Magic

You can use frozen peas here if fresh aren't available, but the flavour of the asparagus hinges on it being in season. If recently picked, it gives off an amazing verdant aroma that really energises the drink. If the asparagus isn't up to the task, replace with a sprig of mint.

START ME UP COCKTAIL

Gather

2 peaches

1 bottle Cocchi Americano

Just under 2 shots (40ml/1.5oz) gin

2 teaspoons apricot brandy

1 teaspoon sugar syrup (see p31)

1 teaspoon aquavit

Small chilled cocktail glass

Cubed ice

Lemon, to garnish

Rob Libecans started in my bar White Lyan after working with the manager Iain in Australia. He's been the source of much hilarity and fun, and as a bonus, some super-tasty cocktails! I always find fresh peaches are one of the best ingredients to pick up from the market when they're in season, and Rob's use of them here goes way beyond more straightforward styles of drink. As the name suggests, it's a great eye-opener too, being crisp and clean despite the nice hit of booze.

Method

Remove the flesh from the peaches. Infuse it in the Cocchi Americano overnight, then strain.

Take a twist of lemon zest using a knife. Add the gin, apricot brandy, sugar syrup, aquavit and just under 1 shot (20ml/0.8oz) peach-infused Cocchi to a mixing glass. Stir over ice, strain into the chilled cocktail glass, and garnish.

Magic

There's a lovely range of herbal and stone-fruit notes in this cocktail, and once you get the hang of their balance, you could vary some of the elements. Pick up peak-season plums or cherries from the market – they add a delicious accent to the drink.

AUTUMN-SPRING SOUR

Gather

½ small butternut, hubbard or delicata squash

300ml/12oz water

200g/8oz sugar

75g/3oz honey

2 shots (50ml/2oz) Springbank 10 year old (or other salty-style single malt)

2 teaspoons lemon juice

1 tablespoon orange juice

6 strands fresh wheatgrass (or if it's clean, regular grass!)

Chilled flute

Cubed ice

This is another amazing vegetal cocktail – essentially a whisky sour at heart – which works so well on autumn evenings. As with the Deadly Nightshade (see p57), it contains an ingredient you might not expect to make its way into your cocktail – squash – but its sweetness balances the saltiness of the whisky. I've taken the route of specifying the spirit here – Springbank is one of my best-loved whiskies, with a unique maritime element that is especially enjoyable in this cocktail. The few strands of wheatgrass lend a little 'garden' bitterness, but use a splash of traditional bitters to tie it all together if you can't get hold of any.

Method

Peel, de-seed and cube the squash. Place in a pot with the water (it should just cover the squash), the sugar and the honey. Bring to the boil, simmer for 15 minutes on a low heat, then remove from the heat. When the mix has cooled, blitz with a blender and pass through a sieve.

Add to a shaker the whisky, lemon, orange, wheatgrass and 1 shot (25ml/1oz) of squash purée (stir, then have a taste – you might need to add a touch more honey depending on the sweetness of your squash). Fill with ice, then shake hard and double strain into your chilled flute (see p27). Add one cube of ice to help it open out.

Magic

Further grassy notes are interesting additions here: you can actually use grass, as mentioned (or even make a grass distillate if you just happen to have some fancy-pants distillation set-up at home!).

However, any 'greener' herbs can be a nice supplement – tarragon or sweet cicely work particularly well. Simply shake them through the mix.

ROCKET TO PLATINO

Gather

2 shots (50ml/2oz) blanco tequila (100% agave)

1 tablespoon Green Chartreuse

1 tablespoon pink grapefruit juice

1 tablespoon lime juice

1 tablespoon sugar syrup (see p31)

Small handful fresh rocket, plus a few leaves to garnish

Small highball

Cubed ice

Chilled soda, to finish

Tequila has an amazing ability to provide some much-needed get-up-and-go when you're feeling the effects of the night before. This cocktail embraces that wholeheartedly, but folds in the peppery green bite of fresh rocket (aka arugula). Pick it up from a farmers' market, as the supermarket stuff really lacks the spice you need. A strong mustardy kick balances the drink.

Method

Tear the rocket and add to a shaker with the booze, lime, grapefruit and syrup. Shake very hard with ice. Double strain over cubed ice in your highball and cap with soda (see p27). Garnish with a few extra leaves of rocket.

Magic

Cherry fits in amazingly here, although you need the dark notes of deep purple fruits – use a couple of fresh ones through the mix. A liqueur such as Cherry Heering works too, or even a spoonful of cherry jam.

SUMMER SOCIAL SIPS

When the weather's good, little get-togethers can swell into parties! You need cocktails that taste great, but are easy to scale up. These pack plenty of seasonal flavour and are light enough for hot weather.

WAGGLEDANCE PUNCH

Gather

1 orange

3 litres/120oz boiling water

3 lemons

3 ripe peaches

8 shots (200ml/8oz) sugar syrup
(see p31)

1 bunch mint

1 bunch lemon verbena

500ml/20oz gin

2 litres/80oz cloudy apple juice

2 bottles chilled prosecco

Punch bowl and cups

This is as fresh as they come: quick to assemble and equally quick to disappear. It's a combination of flavours that just works every time, but it's still complex enough to warrant an extra cup. It's also a showstopping drink to serve and easily caters to a group. When put together properly it bears no resemblance to those frat-boy concoctions that lurk in tubs in the corner of house parties. It's perfect to drink outdoors, and if you don't have a punch bowl, a soup urn or large pot works grand.

Method

To make the orange block, start the day before. Slice the orange thinly and put in an empty ice cream tub or similar. Fill with boiling water, allow to cool and freeze overnight.

Peel then juice the lemons, and stone and slice the peaches. Set the juice and peach aside. Add the lemon peel with the sugar syrup and half the mint and half the verbena leaves to a jug or bowl. Blitz with a stick blender

(or in a food processor), then strain through a sieve.

Add your infused sugar syrup, lemon juice, peach and all the remaining ingredients – except the prosecco – to a punch bowl or soup urn. Mix well (be careful not to tear the herbs). Add the block of orange ice, then the two bottles of prosecco. Stir gently then ladle into cups. Try to get a slice of peach and a few leaves of herbs in each serving.

Magic

For the Waggledance Punch we blitz peels and herbs into the syrup. This extracts lots of flavour, but means the syrup won't last as long – the flavours will fade. No problem here as we use all the syrup at once, but if you want to prep in advance, blanch the herbs by dropping them into boiling water for 10 seconds, then into a bowl of iced water, then wring out and blend into the syrup.

PASS THE BUCK

Gather

2 shots (50ml/2oz) chilled
buckwheat tea

Just under 1 shot (20ml/0.8oz)
grapefruit juice

1 tablespoon elderflower cordial

2 shots (50ml/2oz) blended scotch

Small highball

Cubed ice

Chilled soda, to finish

Grapefruit, to garnish

Lemon, to garnish

I discovered buckwheat tea with my sister Natasha and our 'other sister' Karen when we were visiting Japan together. We drank gallons of the stuff – both hot and cold – and I knew the nutty sweetness would be great paired with a light scotch. Buckwheat is not technically a tea, but makes a lovely brew – you can pick it up from Asian supermarkets under the name 'soba cha'. It makes this drink a great refresher that's also amazing served warm when evenings get a little cool (just omit the soda and ice, and mix with extra tea while it's still hot). This recipe makes one drink, but if you keep to the proportions you can easily scale it up into a pitcher too – just try and use big bits of ice if possible.

Method

Brew a strong pot of buckwheat tea according to the instructions, allow to cool, then strain.

Add 2 shots (50ml/2oz) of tea and everything else (except the soda and grapefruit) to the highball filled with cubed ice. Give it a quick stir, then top with a dash of soda, a slice of grapefruit and a lemon twist.

Magic

You can shake this drink too, omitting the soda and adding an egg white. It becomes a softer, fuller affair but is still really refreshing, given the nice balance of malty notes and the citrus and floral side.

PAISLEY PATTERN PITCHER

Gather

3 lemons

3 tarragon sprigs

6 dashes orange bitters

500ml/20oz Compass Box Asyla
(or light blended scotch)

4 shots (100ml/4oz) elderflower
cordial

5 small highballs

Large ice and cubed ice

Chilled soda, to finish

My memory of cocktail pitchers are pretty hideous – watery ensembles of cheap booze – but when balanced properly they can ease the hassle of supplying a thirsty group. It's a good idea to use big ice cubes, as they'll dilute far slower, giving you time to enjoy: the taste evolves gradually. You can omit the orange bitters, or substitute them for a different bitters you have to hand, but they dry the drink nicely and tie the citrus flavours together. I specifically used Compass Box Asyla whisky as it reminds me of summer – the light, creamy blend created by the company's talented founder John very much guided this drink, so I'd advise seeking it out. However, any delicate blended scotch will work.

Magic

To give the herbal notes a real boost, a couple of dashes of absinthe are terrific in this drink, as is a little mint sprig topping each highball glass.

Method

Using a peeler, take one long piece of zest from around each lemon.

Add the big pieces of ice to a 1.5l/60oz jug or pitcher. Squeeze the lemon zests into it and wrap around the inside. Place in the tarragon. Add the bitters then the scotch and elderflower. Stir well without tearing the herbs and top with chilled soda. Stir carefully, then pour into the highballs filled with cubed ice.

INFUSIONS

The infusions on the next few pages are some of my
favourite combinations - and they make assembling
a tasty drink for summer parties super-simple. They
can be bottled as gifts or kept in the fridge to be
topped with a mixer when your guests arrive.

It's easy to make a fairly big batch to keep for
a while as the alcohol preserves the fruits. After
the fruits have had time to infuse the alcohol (this
usually takes a few hours or up to a day), you need to
strain off the fruit - making sure to get all the small
bits before storing, otherwise it'll continue to infuse and
the batch might taste a little stewed.

Sous vide (water bath) infusions give the best
extraction if you have the means to get all fancy, but a
bit of care and love (and a kilner jar!) is an easy way to
replicate it. Remember to taste as you go, as the
intensity of flavour comes down to your ingredients,
particularly the strength of your booze.

SUMMER BERRY TEQUILA WITH GINGER ALE

Even among those who profess not to like tequila, this drink goes down superbly. The warmth of the aged tequila with the ginger and berries is a great combination that tastes like late summer.

Gather

1 thumb ginger

Punnet of blackberries

Punnet of raspberries

Punnet of strawberries

4 shots (100ml/4oz) water

4 shots (100ml/4oz) cider vinegar

100g/4oz sugar

1 bottle reposado tequila

Highball

Cubed ice

Good-quality, chilled ginger ale, to finish

Rosemary sprig, to garnish

Method

Wash the ginger and chop the unpeeled ginger. Wash the berries, removing the leaves from the strawberries.

Add the ginger, berries, water, vinegar and sugar to a pan and bring to the boil. When the berries have begun to break down, simmer for 5 minutes, then stir. Remove from the heat and allow to cool.

Add the fruit mixture to a big jar together with the bottle of tequila and stir well again. Allow to infuse for a few hours (or up to a day) and strain through a sieve. Store in the fridge.

To serve, fill a highball with cubed ice and add 2 shots (50ml/2oz) of the infusion. Top with chilled ginger ale, stir and add a sprig of rosemary.

Magic

Once you're comfortable with the flavours, you can start to build in accent notes in the garnish or in the infusion – I've even cooked down sourdough bread with this for a marvellous malty note. The Summer Berry Tequila has a real warmth, but varying the vinegar can add a subtle twist too – raspberry vinegar works incredibly well.

GRAPEFRUIT AND ROSEMARY GIN WITH GINGER ALE

Gather

3 grapefruits

100g/4oz sugar

2 rosemary sprigs

1 bottle London dry gin

Small highball

Cubed ice

Chilled ginger ale, to finish

Grapefruit or orange, to garnish

This is my personal spin on a gin buck – it has one of my favourite citrus fruits and one of my favourite herbs, and they're balanced perfectly. The grapefruit lends a big bold tang to the gin, while the rosemary gives a summery, herbal edge. Tonic would be a good mixer too, but here with ginger ale, the balance really shines.

Method

Zest the grapefruits using a peeler.

Add the peel along with the sugar, rosemary and gin to a large jar and stir until the sugar is dissolved. Allow to infuse for a few hours (or up to a day) and strain through a sieve. Store in the fridge.

To serve, fill a highball with cubed ice and add 2 shots (50ml/2oz) of the infusion. Top with chilled ginger ale, stir and add a slice of grapefruit.

Magic

You can add the whole sliced flesh of the grapefruit to the infusion jar for a plumper flavour, but it can taste a little tired after a while, so make sure to drink it quick if you go down this route. The zest is a great provider of flavour, but you can also add combined citrus notes to complement the gin: lemon with grapefruit works with fresher styles such as Bombay Sapphire, while orange with grapefruit is excellent for warmer, spicier ones like Tanqueray or No 3.

PEACH AND SAGE BOURBON

This is heading towards julep territory but is a nice savoury/sweet combination which is delicious on its own over ice. You can lengthen as needs be, but it's perfect with some bites to eat (toasted almonds are awesome with this) or when you need something rich and sweet in the early evening.

Gather

3 shots (75ml/3oz) honey
(wildflower honey is perfect)

1 bottle bourbon

3 ripe peaches

2 stems sage

1 large jar

Small rocks glass

Cubed ice

Orange, to garnish

Method

Add the honey and bourbon to a jar and stir until dissolved. Tear the flesh from the peaches and place with their stone kernels in the jar. Add the sage and stir gently. Allow to infuse for a few hours (or up to a day). Strain through a sieve and store in the fridge.

To serve, fill a rocks glass with ice and add 2 shots (50ml/2oz) of infusion. Using the peeler, cut a strip of orange zest, twist over the glass and drop in.

Magic

Burnt peach and bourbon are also amazing together: they take this drink in a slightly different direction, but a delicious direction nonetheless. Char or grill the peaches then follow as above. An additional flavour – such as cinnamon – can also work great: just don't put too much in.

ELDERFLOWER AND CHOCOLATE SCOTCH WITH SODA

Gather

15g/0.5oz cocoa nibs

1 bottle blended scotch

100ml/4oz elderflower liqueur
(or cordial)

Small highball

Cubed ice

Chilled soda water, to finish

Small bunch of mint, to garnish

This cocktail is more about the pairing of the floral elderflower and nutty chocolate than the scotch, but the whisky does far more than just act as a slug of booze. It works better than alternative spirits because the sweetness of its malt and grain balances the mix. Use a lighter style to save the flavour becoming too heavy for a highball serve: you want this fresh and summery. On that note, the peachy/melon flavours of elderflower liqueur are sometimes better than the sharpness of cordial.

Method

Add the nibs to a dry frying pan and heat. Keep the pan moving and gently toast them until they take on a light gloss. Transfer to a large jar and add the scotch and elderflower liqueur. Infuse for a few hours (or up to a day). Strain through a sieve and store in the fridge.

To serve, fill a highball with cubed ice and add 2 shots (50ml/2oz) of the infusion. Top with soda, stir and garnish with the mint.

Magic

This also makes a delicious take on a mojito – serve long over cracked ice with 1 shot (25ml/1oz) lemon juice and some mint leaves.

PINEAPPLE RUM
WITH GINGER BEER

Gather

1 bottle golden rum

50g/2oz sugar

1 thumb ginger

1 very ripe pineapple

Small highball

Cubed ice

Chilled, good-quality ginger beer

Lime, to garnish

Pineapple rum is super-delicious. The key is finding a style of rum that sings along with the golden, tropical notes of the fruit – an aged rum is great and even more ideal if it has a fruity profile itself. Something like Bacardi 8 or Plantation 5 is perfect, but you can take a grassier style such as Havana Club on if you want the whole thing a little less sweet.

Method

Mix the rum and sugar in a jar. Peel and chop the ginger and pineapple and add to the sweetened rum. Allow to infuse for a few hours (or up to a day). Strain through a sieve and store in the fridge.

To serve, fill a highball with cubed ice and add 2 shots (50ml/2oz) of the infusion. Top with chilled ginger beer, stir and add a couple of squeezed wedges of lime.

Magic

A very ripe fruit is vital here – if you try to pick up the pineapple by a leaf and it pulls out, you're on the right track. It should smell of ripe fruit before it's cut, too. If you know you're going to drink this cocktail quickly (with friends round you will, it's damn delicious), simply blitz the ripe pineapple into the rum. Cardamom is also a great companion to pineapple – the seeds of one pod is plenty to add.

ST CLEMENTS COGNAC WITH GINGER BEER

Gather

100g/4oz sugar

1 bottle cognac

3 lemons

2 oranges

1 star anise

Small highball

Cubed ice

Chilled, good-quality ginger beer

Lemon, to garnish

Go for a lighter Borderies style of VS or VSOP cognac here, to play up to the fruitier, citrussy notes. The ginger beer gives more of an evening warmth, but you can use lighter mixers if you wish.

Method

Add the sugar and cognac to a large jar and stir until dissolved. Peel the citrus in long lengths then add to the jar with the star anise. Allow to infuse for a few hours (or up to a day) and strain through a sieve. Store in the fridge.

To serve, fill a highball with cubed ice and add 2 shots (50ml/2oz) of the infusion. Top with ginger beer, stir and add a squeezed wedge of lemon.

Magic

You can cook down the citrus peels to more of a marmalade consistency for a more intense flavour – simply slice and boil with the sugar and a splash of water. If you're taking this option, thinly slice some citrus into wheels and dry in a low oven overnight into citrus crisps to garnish. This gives a much more brooding version of the drink that would suit a darker, more leathery style of cognac.

RHUBARB, PEAR AND CARDAMOM VODKA WITH FRESH LEMONADE

Gather

100g/4oz sugar

1 bottle vodka

1 green cardamom pod

1 black cardamom pod

1 stick rhubarb

2 pears

Small highball

Cubed ice

Lemon, to finish

Chilled soda water, to finish

You can simply infuse this in a pitcher for a lighter and fresher style, or allow a longer maceration and strain out the bulk for a blush-pink, aromatic spirit. The black cardamom adds a eucalyptus-style verve to the typical spice of the green stuff. The pear and rhubarb create a nicely tart infusion which is awesome with the zest of the lemonade.

Method

Stir the sugar into the vodka in a large jar. Gently press and toast the cardamom pods in a frying pan over a low heat until they begin to release their aroma, then add to the vodka.

Slice the rhubarb and pears and add to the mix and allow to infuse for a few hours (or up to a day). Strain through a sieve and store in the fridge.

To serve, fill a highball with cubed ice and add 2 shots (50ml/2oz) of the infusion. Squeeze the juice of half a lemon into the glass, stir and top with chilled soda. You might need a touch of sugar syrup for balance.

Magic

You can cook the pears and rhubarb in some water and sugar to draw out a bolder flavour. Simply add to a pan on low heat and warm until the rhubarb breaks down, allow to cool, then strain and add into the vodka. Follow the rest of the recipe as normal.

JULEP

There's a whole world of debate surrounding how to make the Julep. But this is the simplest, tastiest and easiest method to cater for family and friends.

Juleps were designed as cooling drinks, early-evening sippers with the freshness of the mint easing into the sweet bourbon as it slowly dilutes over cracked ice. And the consistency of the ice is what really makes the Julep so interesting. The drink should start nice and sweet then gradually mellow out as the ice melts. Snow-cone ice is going too far - simply crack some fresh ice to allow your drink a good journey from first sip to last.

MINT JULEP

Gather

1 bunch mint

1 fresh peach (or the kernels of 2 –
see *Magic*, below)

100g/4oz sugar

1 bottle bourbon

2 slithers of cassia bark

6 chilled metal cups

Cubed ice

Mint, to garnish

This is my favourite take on the classic. Mint and sweet bourbon are cooling in a tried-and-tested way, but the peach and cassia here accent perfectly. This should be made up in a batch, with some small (ideally pewter) cups sitting chilling alongside in the fridge. When friends come round, simply crack some ice, pour a good serve and pick some fresh mint (spanked to release the fragrance). If you're lucky enough to have a garden, I expect you already have a fresh batch chilling away – this is exactly what you want to be sipping lazily in the sun.

Method

Wash and pick the mint, discarding any browning leaves. Tear the peach flesh from the kernel.

Mix the sugar and bourbon in a large jar, then add the peach, cassia and mint, stems-side up. Gently swirl the mint but be extra careful not to tear it. Leave to infuse in the fridge for 3 hours, then stir again and strain.

To serve, fold cubed ice into a clean tea towel and give it a few sound cracks with a rolling pin (or something sturdy that won't shatter in your hand). The ice should be just broken so that it melts quickly, but not so fast that you have to chug your drink.

Put the cracked ice in a chilled cup and add 3 shots (75ml/3oz) of mix. Churn gently (not too much or else the drink will peak too soon). Cap with more ice. Place in a couple of straws, slap a big bouquet of mint and position beside the straws.

Magic

Be vigilant of browning mint or of tearing the leaves. The enzymatic effect of less-than-fresh leaves and the release of chlorophyll from torn ones just make for a bitter aftertaste – you don't want this. For a nuttier take, use leftover peach kernels (with a little flesh left on), which gives a lovely almond note that elevates the bourbon perfectly.

GULAB JULEP

Gather

1 bottle vodka

1 teaspoon rosewater

100g/4oz white sugar

1 bunch mint

15g/0.5oz cocoa nibs

6 chilled metal cups

Cubed ice

Mint, to garnish

The additions here might lead you to believe this is a very saccharine version of a julep, but it's wonderfully clean, retaining that essential cooling effect. Go easy on the rosewater though; with potent ingredients – particularly floral ones that can taste like pot-pourri in big doses – less is more. Choose your vodka carefully too. Many think of vodka as a blank slate, but when looking at good-quality spirits (and of course, go for the best you can, always), there are many nuances to ponder. Use a potato-based spirit such as Luksusowa or Chase and you'll end up with a creamier version of this drink, whereas a grain-based such as Ketel One, Belvedere or Grey Goose will carry a nuttiness through to the end.

Method

In a jar mix the vodka, rosewater and sugar until dissolved.

Wash and pick the mint for any browning leaves. Gently toast the cocoa nibs in a dry pan. When glossy, add to a large jar along with the mint, stems pointing up. Leave to infuse in the fridge for 3 hours, then stir again and strain.

To serve, fold some fresh ice in a tea towel and give it a few whacks with a rolling pin (or another sturdy bludgeon that won't shatter in your hand).

The ice should just be broken – as with all these Juleps, the ice should dilute quickly but not so fast you end up with a glass of water.

Put the cracked ice in a chilled cup and add 3 shots (75ml/3oz) of mix. Churn gently (again, not too much or the drink will peak too soon) and cap with more ice. Place a couple of straws in, slap a big bouquet of mint and place alongside.

Magic

Add a little twist from a peppermill over the top of the drink. Too much will make you sneeze, but a little aromatic pepper is a lovely foil to the fragrance of the rose and mint.

DEATH BY JULEP

Gather

1 bunch mint

3 stems oregano

100g/4oz unrefined sugar

1 bottle reposado tequila

6 chilled metal cups

Cubed ice

Mint, to garnish

Tequila is great at mealtimes, so when I was working on a Mexican food-and-drink project called Death by Burrito with my chef buddy Shay, this was our signature. It's got similar notes to many of the dishes we served, but the freshness of the mint cuts through some of the more pungent spices. I don't do spicy food (at all – I'm a real pansy about it), but a touch of chilli is actually lovely in this too.

Method

Wash and pick the mint and oregano for any browning leaves. Mix the sugar in a jar with the tequila until dissolved. Add the mint and oregano, stems-side pointing up. Leave to infuse in the fridge for 3 hours, then stir again and strain through a sieve.

To serve, fold some fresh and dry ice in a clean tea towel and give it a few hits with a rolling pin (or something else sturdy that won't shatter in your hand).

You only need a few good cracks. The ice should just be broken so that it melts quickly, but not so fast that the drink becomes watery.

Put the cracked ice in a chilled cup, and add 3 shots (75ml/3oz) of mix. Churn gently (not too much else the drink will arc too soon). Cap with more ice then place a couple of straws in, slap a big bouquet of mint and place beside the straws.

Magic

Tequila is misunderstood. Try different variants – blanco, reposado, anejo – and different brands. Something punchy and young such as Tapatio Blanco makes for a peppery take, while aged Siete Leguas Reposado leads to a softer, more golden version.

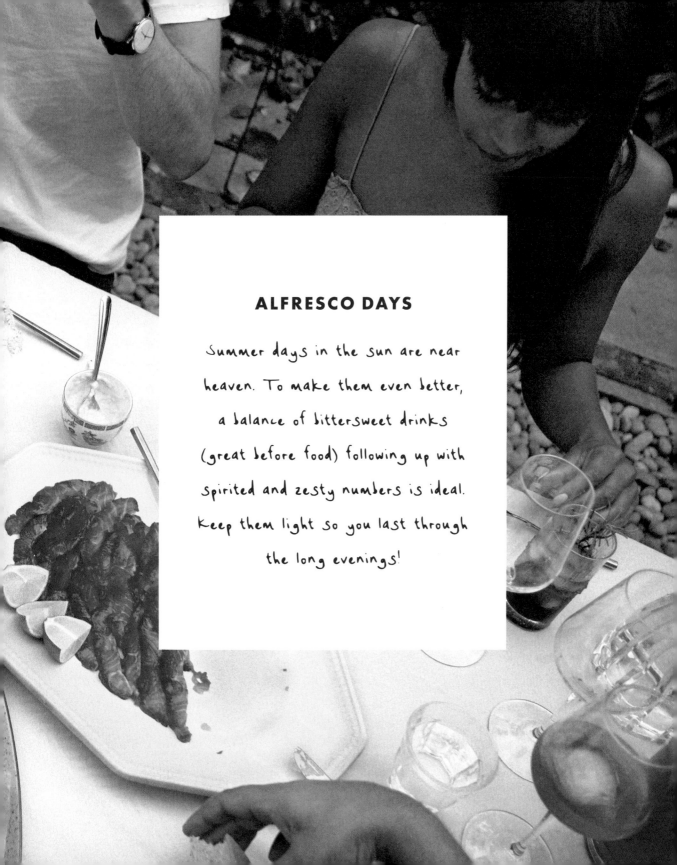

ALFRESCO DAYS

Summer days in the sun are near
heaven. To make them even better,
a balance of bittersweet drinks
(great before food) following up with
spirited and zesty numbers is ideal.
Keep them light so you last through
the long evenings!

AMERICANO

Gather

Just over 1 shot (30ml/1.2oz) chilled Campari

Just over 1 shot (30ml/1.2oz) chilled sweet vermouth

Highball

Cubed ice

Chilled soda, to finish

Rosemary sprig, to garnish

If it hits early evening and you know you have a big meal ahead, you need an Americano – it's simple to assemble and is the perfect light, bittersweet aperitif. A full-bodied, sweet vermouth works best, but you can vary according to mood. I'd shy away from using the bitter styles here, such as Punt e Mes, as the bite of the Campari really shines through: too much is overkill. The charred rosemary is a simple flourish, but creates an aroma that reminds me of barbecues in the sun, and links perfectly into the drink. Remember you want the soda to be fresh too – sparkle and pop is an absolute must.

Method

Holding the rosemary sprig at the base (fingers don't smell very pleasant when torched!), gently pass over the flame, charring the leaves until they're smoking and releasing their wonderful fragrance.

Fill a narrow highball with ice cubes and add the Campari and vermouth. Stir, add more ice, top with soda then pop in the burnt rosemary.

Magic

You can pre-mix a blend of Campari and vermouth (in equal proportions) and bottle, and simply keep in an ice bucket with some soda if you're making a number of these outdoors.

BICYCLETTA

Gather

2 lemons

500ml/20oz boiling water

4 shots (100ml/4oz) white wine
(something nice and crisp)

Just over 1 shot (30ml/1.2oz) Campari

Wine glass

Big ice cubes or lemon ice (see Method)

Orange, to garnish

This is an ideal drink to share with one or two friends early evening where you can enjoy the drink in a relaxed setting – you just need access to your fridge and freezer. Here, I've taken the simple combination of crisp white wine and Campari and twisted it with the addition of flavoured ice. As it melts it opens everything out and adds a vibrant layer to each sip. It's super-easy to do – just make sure to have some prepped the day before.

Method

To make lemon ice, remove the zest of a couple of lemons with a peeler. Steep in the boiling water. Wait for it to cool, then strain. Pour into an ice cube tray or silicon moulds and freeze. You can pop a small piece of lemon peel in each cube as it's freezing if you want an extra aesthetic element.

Cut a piece of orange zest using a peeler.

Put some lemon ice (or regular ice) into a wine glass, add the wine and Campari and stir briefly. Snap the strip of orange peel over the top and drop in.

Magic

A little touch of fruit liqueur (just a teaspoon or so) such as Cointreau, poire or cassis is a lovely addition. But your wine needs to be clean and dry to stop the drink becoming too thick.

DIAMOND RICKEY

Gather

2 shots (50ml/2oz) Mr Lyan
Diamond Rickey

Chilled Fever-Tree Mediterranean tonic

Tumbler

Cubed ice

Grapefruit, to garnish

Thyme, to garnish

Mint, to garnish

Rosemary, to garnish

There's nothing quite like a good G&T at the end of a long day. The sharp gin and the bite of the tonic slowly develop over time to help you ease away the troubles of the day. This is a simple version that adds a little touch of magic. Distilled grapefruit and lime are folded into gin in my bottled Diamond Rickey along with a touch of falernum – a light lime and almond liqueur – leading to a more involving serve. I've matched it with Fever-Tree's Mediterranean tonic here which provides a lovely herbal bite.

Method

Fill your glass with ice cubes, add the Rickey and top with tonic. Garnish with a slice of grapefruit and a sprig of thyme, mint and rosemary, and enjoy a moment of relaxation.

Magic

If you don't have the Diamond Rickey to hand, use two tablespoons of gin, a tablespoon of lime and a splash of sugar syrup. Regular tonic will also work well if you can't find the Mediterranean version, or try this with bitter lemon.

BOTTLED COSMO

Gather

1 lemon

3 limes

4 shots (100ml/4oz) cranberry juice

12 shots (300ml/12oz) citrus vodka

8 shots (200ml/8oz) Cointreau

1 teaspoon orange bitters

2 (fresh or dried) bay leaves

Bottle

Highball

Cubed ice

Chilled ginger ale, to finish

Orange, to garnish

Lavender sprigs, to garnish

If your friends are anything like mine, a gathering at the house can be a little hard to organise, so removing as many difficulties as possible is a plus. This is a very welcome variation on the Cosmopolitan that seems to suit all palates, and leads to a brisk, dry yet fruity serve that's easy to put together. Simply take the bottle outside with some ice, glasses and chilled ginger ale and let everyone help themselves.

Method

To make the Bottled Cosmo mix, take 1 strip of lemon zest and 3 strips of lime zest using a peeler, and juice the limes with a hand-squeezer.

Mix the peels, citrus juice, cranberry, booze, bitters and bay leaves in a large jug. Rest for at least 10 minutes, then strain and pour into a clean bottle. Cap and keep well chilled.

To serve, fill a narrow highball with ice and add 2 shots (50ml/2oz) Bottled Cosmo mix. Cut a strip of orange peel using a peeler. Top with chilled ginger ale, and garnish with the orange twist and a lavender sprig.

Magic

This will serve eight to ten people and will keep in the fridge for two days. If you can allow the peels and bay leaves to infuse for a few hours, all the better.

MULBERRY SMASH

Gather

2 teaspoons mulberry jam

2 shots (50ml/2oz) gin

1 shot (25ml/1oz) lemon

8 mint leaves

Rocks glass

Cubed ice

Cracked ice

Mint sprig, to garnish

Blueberries or mulberries, to garnish

Homemade syrups are an easy and handy way of getting interesting flavours into your drinks (see p31), but many items from the kitchen cupboard are ideal for adding a unique spin too. Jams may seem obvious, but are excellent all the same. I recently discovered mulberry jam, which has a wonderful vanilla-berry sweetness that isn't too cloying. Depending on the sweetness of the jam (or the tartness of your lemons) you might still need a splash of sugar. Like the name Mulberry Smash suggests, all the flavours of this drink are literally pounded together, hence why it's served over cracked ice – this lets everything unfold and dilute.

Method

Stir the jam into the gin at the bottom of a shaker, then add all the other ingredients and shake hard with ice.

Double strain over cracked ice in a rocks glass (see p27). Garnish with a sprig of mint and some blueberries (or fresh mulberries, if you can get some).

Magic

The base works with many spirits, so you can substitute the alcohol to match your jam. Of course you can vary it all depending on the jams and preserves you have in your fridge, and just experiment to match complementary flavours.

PEACH AND VERBENA SMASH

Gather

1 peach

2 lemon verbena sprigs

1 shot (25ml/1oz) lemon juice

1 tablespoon sugar syrup (see p31)

Just over 2 shots (60ml/2.4oz) white rum

Rocks glass

Cubed ice

I love having verbena in my garden – it's an easy-to-grow herb with a citrussy taste, and makes an amazing hot infusion. This cocktail makes outstanding use of verbena to complement fresh peach (you'll notice peaches popping up a lot in this book – I always make the most of them when they're around). This Peach and Verbena Smash is a white rum sour at heart, but one that reflects the best of fresh produce. I'd suggest getting yourself a little verbena plant – it'll do fine on a windowsill – and as well as being brilliant in cocktails and tea, it can be used in savoury and sweet cooking. You can pick the herb up from shops too though.

Method

Cut the peach from the stone, saving a slice for garnish.

Fold some ice in a tea towel and smack into cracked pieces with a rolling pin.

Take half the peach and muddle in a shaker. Add 1 sprig of verbena, the lemon, sugar and rum. Shake hard with cubed ice: you need to essentially smash the peach and verbena. Double strain over cracked ice into your rocks glass (see p27), then garnish with the peach slice and the other verbena sprig.

Magic

If you have a blender to hand, you can blitz this up with a handful of cracked ice. It's essentially a boozy slushy: a frozen drink which will really hit the spot on a hot day.

RAINY DAY SPRITZ

Gather

1 shot (25ml/1oz) Mr Lyan
Rainy Day Spritz

2 shots (50ml/2oz) dry white wine

Wine glass

Cubed ice

2 shots (50ml/2oz) chilled soda, to finish

2 raspberries, to garnish

Grapefruit, to garnish

This is a cocktail I enjoyed at my dad's place by the coast down in Devon when we had some unseasonably lovely autumn weather. It's ideal on a late afternoon when there's just a brief moment to have something bracing outdoors. If you're after a more celebratory version, just substitute the white wine for a sparkling wine. It feels summery either way, so will transport you even if the best of the year's sunshine has passed.

I created my bottled cocktails so people could enjoy true cocktails in different settings and without any of the faff or fuss. They're also awesome bases – they're complex mixes, so you don't have to lug around several bottles. There's little to mess up with this one: it has a beautiful balance of raspberry, rhubarb and vermouth, with just enough dryness.

Method

Cut a strip of grapefruit zest using a peeler.

Fill wine glass with ice and add the Spritz and wine. Stir, add ice, then top with the soda. Garnish with the raspberries and the twist.

Magic

Aperol makes for a classic spritz if you don't have a bottle of Mr Lyan Rainy Day Spritz, or instead try substituting it with some vermouth or raspberry liqueur.

PRE-DINNER

If you have friends coming
for dinner, serve a drink that doesn't
knock them for six as they come
through the door, but sets up their
palates - and bellies - for what
you've prepared in the kitchen.

GIN BASIL FIX

Gather

1 Thai basil sprig

1 shot (25ml/1oz) gin

1 shot (25ml/1oz) crème de poire

1 tablespoon lemon juice

Small highball

Cubed ice

Chilled soda, to finish

This is a great pre-dinner cocktail, that's both zesty and fresh: it's for those who won't go near bitter drinks. It was actually created on the roof of my sister Natasha's apartment in New York before we had dinner. She had a little garden going with some great stuff flourishing in the sun, including super-pungent Thai basil. Thai basil leans more towards anise than its European cousin and so cosies up close with the notes from the gin and pear liqueur. I love this as an aperitif as it's just so clean – and was perfectly suited when we ate with my close friend, the incredible chef Seamus Mullen (who completely coincidentally now rents Natasha's flat!).

Method

Gently slap the basil to release some of the scent (without bruising or tearing it), then place in the highball glass.

Add the gin, crème de poire and lemon. Stir gently, then fill with cubed ice. Stir, pull the basil up from the bottom with a spoon, and crown with a splash of soda.

Magic

A small dash of absinthe gives the anise of the basil a bit of a helping hand. The best thing is to either use a dropper, or a small spray bottle, to give a 'rinse' – less is more in this scenario. Of course, if you don't have any Thai basil, regular basil proves a worthy stand-in; or even try another soft herb such as coriander.

BLOODY EARNEST

This was another cocktail created at my sister Natasha's apartment, in this case to make the most of the amazing tomatoes she was growing. It ended up as an agreeably perky aperitif. A simple twist on a Hemingway Daiquiri, it has a lingering savoury note. Red grapefruits are ideal here, but pink will be just fine if you can't find one. Don't bother adding the tomato if they aren't in season; without their sweetly acidic kick they're just not worth it.

Gather

1 small tomato such as a cherry or pomodorino, plus 1 to garnish

Just under 1 shot (20ml/0.8oz) red grapefruit juice

2 teaspoons lime juice

2 teaspoons sugar syrup (see p31)

1 teaspoon maraschino liqueur

Just over 2 shots (60ml/2.4oz) white rum

Chilled coupette glass

Cubed ice

Grapefruit, to garnish

Method

Cut a small strip of grapefruit zest using a peeler and set aside.

Crush the tomato in the bottom of a shaker, then add all the other ingredients.

Fill with ice and shake hard. Double strain into a chilled cocktail glass (see p27). Twist a little grapefruit peel over the top and add a tomato for garnish.

Magic

Daiquiris need to be blisteringly cold, so shake the hell out of this one. You can crack a little ice into the tin to assist with this. You might want to wrap it all in a tea towel to keep your hands from freezing – the outside of the tin should be frosted.

If you can't get good tomatoes, try shaking a couple of olive leaves (you can buy them dried) through the drink – it'll give a similar light, piquant note.

VERMOUTH COCKTAIL

Gather

1 teaspoon lemon blossom syrup

1 teaspoon raspberry syrup

1 dash orange bitters

1 dash Angostura bitters

Just over 1 shot (30ml/1.2oz) Cocchi Americano, Lillet Blanc or dry vermouth

Just over 1 shot (30ml/1.2oz) Martini Rosso or sweet vermouth

Chilled cocktail glass

Cubed ice

Lemon, to garnish

Vermouth is brilliant to have in the house, not just because it's so suited to sipping before or with dinner. Cocktails such as this are excellent to have in your arsenal as they help you use up your vermouth while it's still fresh (always store it in the fridge, too). I make my own lemon blossom syrup while my tree is in bloom (don't use all the blossom, or you'll get no lemons!), but it isn't essential – just use an additional lemon zest. You can also make your own raspberry syrup: rest a punnet of raspberries in a fresh batch of sugar syrup as it's cooling, then press it all through a sieve. Or, there are some very decent ones on the market now.

Method

Add all the ingredients to a mixing glass. Stir, fill with cubed ice and stir again for around 20 seconds. Cut a small piece of lemon peel. Strain into a chilled cocktail glass and twist the peel over the top.

Magic

There are endless variables with this wonderfully refreshing cocktail. Try sherries or other fortified wines instead of the vermouth, swap out the syrups or the bitters for different varieties, or stir through herbs or spices… Just think about the food you're serving and you'll have a blast.

REPOSADO HIGHBALL

Gather

1½ shots (40ml/1.5oz) reposado tequila

1 tablespoon Lillet Blanc

1 dash Angostura bitters (optional)

Small highball

Cubed ice

Chilled ginger ale, to finish

Mint sprig, to garnish

This long mix is a fine partner for light bites, but it also works brilliantly as an early-evening cocktail which reveals hidden nuances as it dilutes. It's a wonderfully golden highball that really shows off the sweet spice of a lightly aged tequila. Aim for a bottle that says '100% agave' (the succulent Mexican plant that's used to make tequila) and states 'reposado' (rested) rather than one that's simply golden. You'll really notice the difference.

Method

Fill a glass with ice and add the tequila and Lillet (and the bitters, if you want a drier drink). Stir, add more ice and top with the ginger ale. Spank your mint and place alongside a straw in the glass.

Magic

Lillet Blanc is a fabulously honeyed wine-based aperitif that marries up with the tequila perfectly, but you can substitute it for different complementary partners – think anything light or herbal. Kamm & Sons, Suze, dry vermouth or Cocchi Americano are all amazing here, and provide that all-essential pre-dinner appetite-rousing bite!

BITTER BUBBLES

1 grapefruit

1 tablespoon Campari

Chilled flute

Chilled champagne, to finish

Grapefruit, to finish

Bubbles and bitter things – ideal pre-meal sips that sit so well with snacks, canapés and nibbles. It's a decidedly grown-up combination, and is best served as guests start to arrive. There's been so many riffs on these base ingredients throughout drinking history, and many a classic is based upon this combination, but sometimes keeping it very simple is all that's needed. You can vary it around what ingredients you have to hand at the time, or what food you're serving. Fruity or herbal notes can be nice additions, or ramp up the digestive qualities with a small dash of complementary bitters.

Method

Peel and trim a strip of grapefruit zest. Pour the Campari in the flute. Twist the grapefruit over the top and wrap around the inside of the glass. Top with champagne. Here's a tip: don't measure the champagne using a shot glass or jigger, as this will knock the bubbles out. Most (normal-sized!) flutes hold around 125ml/5oz, so roughly 4 shots (100ml/4oz) – leaving a good gap at the top of the glass, of course – should create the balance you're looking for.

Magic

I actually find Campari quite sweet, so I welcome a little extra bitterness. One of my favourite enhancements here is to soak cardamom or celery seeds in some vodka or neutral grain spirit and add a drop to the drink. If you want to go the opposite route and sweeten things up, a splash of cassis is lovely.

COCHIN COOLER

Gather

1 teaspoon cardamom tea
(or 1 green cardamom pod and
1 teaspoon loose-leaf black tea)

12 shots (300ml/12oz)
London dry gin

350ml/12.4oz water

500g/20oz sugar

Handful lemon leaves, shredded (or 2
tablespoons dried lemon leaves or a few
stems of lemongrass or lemongrass tea)

Pinch sea salt

Bottle

Frozen flute

Chilled Fever-Tree ginger ale, to finish

Lemongrass stem, to garnish

I love highballs as aperitifs as they work so well to have a chat over, while also setting your palate up ahead of dinner. I always had go-tos for this, but after travelling to India to visit where the finest ginger is grown, I looked at the spice very differently, and wanted to celebrate the zestier side to the root when it's grown with real care and expertise. I can tell you that this is captured in the ginger ale from Fever-Tree so you don't have to go to the painful lengths of sourcing the best ginger! Serving this very cold, and in a flute, highlights the effervescence and the citrus side of the spice, and still works as a pre-dinner style. There's a different kind of elegance and profile here compared to the classic highball or gin buck serve. All the ingredients nod to demonstrating the wider range of flavours present when you use spices fresh, so get the best you can, and make a note to test and change your spices regularly, so that they're at their brightest!

Method

Add the tea to the gin and infuse in the fridge for 2 hours, then strain.

Make the lemon syrup by heating the water until boiling, remove from the heat then add the sugar and the lemon leaves. Stir to dissolve, then allow to cool. Strain and keep in a clean container in the fridge until needed.

Mix the salt into the water, then add the gin and 2 shots (50ml/2oz) of the lemon leaf syrup. Add to a bottle and store in the freezer for at least 2 hours.

Add a shot and half (40ml/1.5oz) of the gin mix to the frozen flute, top with the ginger ale, then garnish with the lemongrass stem.

Magic

Temperature plays a key role in the profile of the drink. By making everything super cold, we subdue the sweetness, and the heat of the ginger – allowing the citrussy, greener side of the ginger and the gin (I lean to the balance of Beefeater London Dry here, but the fruity pop of Porter's Tropical Old Tom is also a great option) to come to the fore. The temperature also keeps the bubbles in the mix smaller and fresher, and means the drink has a cleaner profile that's perfect ahead of dinner.

FRIDAY NIGHTS

Post-work drinks at home can be
just what's needed to relax and soothe.
Conversely, sometimes you need a
little livener that will lift your fatigue
ahead of a night out – something with
more pep than beer or wine!

CHOCOLATE WINE

Gather

1 bottle red wine (something fruity, not too tannic)

100g/4oz sugar

10g/0.4oz cocoa nibs

Pinch anise seeds

Small pinch sea salt

3 black peppercorns

30g/1oz dried apricots

6 shots (150ml/6oz) cognac

Wine glass

Cubed ice

Chilled soda, to finish (optional)

This is as delicious as its name suggests, although much less sweet than you might imagine. It's incredible as a standalone early-evening cocktail, or with some lightly sweet-savoury dishes. You won't use this whole batch in a single sitting, so you can keep it chilled in the fridge for those times you get home and just need to curl up with a red wine but want that little something more.

Method

Add all ingredients to a microwave-safe bowl, stir, and cover with cling film/plastic food wrap. Heat on high power in the microwave for 3 minutes. Allow to cool, then strain. Keep the apricots: they'll taste boozy but great!

To serve, pour a small wineglass-worth (5 shots/125ml/5oz) over ice. Stir and cap with more ice, although you could simply serve it chilled minus the ice. A splash of soda will lighten it if your wine is particularly heavy.

Magic

This recipe is a great base, but you can layer in further flavours with ease – it's fairly robust. I wouldn't add too many new things at once, but I have varied this several times with fantastic results. I once planned to serve it with roast lamb, so I threw in a couple of pinches of fennel seed and a sliced fresh carrot to the mix (really!) and it matched the food spectacularly well.

BUBBLES AND BYASS

Gather

Just over 2 shots (60ml/2.4oz) fino sherry

1 tablespoon apricot liqueur

1 stem fresh basil

Wine glass

Cubed ice

Chilled soda water, to finish

Green olives, to garnish

As I've already professed, I love dry sherries – a chilled glassful with some olives in the sun and I'm set – but it's also amazing as a base in cocktails. Basil, apricot and sherry is a holy trinity of ingredients to me, and I've used it in several concoctions over the years. The apricot draws out a real warmth from the wine before the basil brings it back round into savoury territory, making it ideal for an early-evening cocktail. And it's still ideal with olives.

I really bonded with Seamus Mullen over our love of sherry, and I couldn't think of a more fitting complement to his awesome cooking than this light (yet complex) ode to sherry cocktails.

Method

To the wine glass, add some ice and the sherry, apricot and basil. Stir gently. Add more ice then a splash of soda, and garnish with a couple of olives.

Magic

Vanilla is an element that can elevate this drink to really special levels. It can be difficult, however, to extract creaminess without the flavour becoming overpowering. One of the best ways is to split a vanilla pod and infuse in a bottle of sherry overnight, then strain and use as above. Save the pod for making vanilla salt or sugar.

PALOMA

Tequila gives you zing! It's a spirit I immediately reach for ahead of a night out; it reminds me of past celebrations, and it combines so well with other zesty ingredients that you can't help but feel perked up. And forget any negative memories of bad tequila: grab a bottle of the real stuff (100% agave) and give this cocktail a go. I love the life it gets from a good old shaking, but if you're making for a big group you can build it in the glass too. The savoury note in the tequila means it pairs brilliantly with food, too.

Gather

1 pinch pink salt (Himalayan, not curing salt)

1 tablespoon lime juice

1 tablespoon pink grapefruit juice

1 tablespoon sugar syrup (see p31)

2 shots (50ml/2oz) blanco tequila (100% agave)

Small highball

Cubed ice

Chilled soda, to finish

Grapefruit, to garnish

Method

Add all the ingredients to a shaker and short-shake over cubed ice (just a couple of quick blasts; this drink is served long so doesn't need to be diluted too much at this stage). Double strain into an ice-filled highball (see p27). Crown with a splash of soda and garnish with a slice of grapefruit.

Magic

On occasion I've served this at parties, carbonated from a syphon: simply add all the mix (around 8 serves) plus 2 shots (50ml/2oz) of water per serve to a syphon and charge with CO_2. Gently dispense over ice. Also, a couple of other flavours such as raspberry or basil can be added to great effect. You can even try topping the drink with lager instead of soda, which produces a pleasant malty bitterness and only boosts food-matching cred.

OLD FASHIONED

Gather

1 or 2 teaspoons sugar syrup
(depending on the sweetness of your
bourbon, and tooth – see p31)

2 dashes Angostura bitters

Just over 2 shots (60ml/2.4oz) bourbon

Rocks glass

Cubed ice

Big pieces of ice

Orange, to garnish

Old Fashioneds are intense and heady – perfect after a meal, or for when you need something bold to kick back with. It's not a complex cocktail (despite the rumour that it takes 15 minutes to make properly) and is as suited to serving a big group as well as just for you and a friend. Try to have big pieces of ice that fit snugly in your glass – this will ensure you're not left with a watery mess. Add the bourbon in two stages – the short final stir releases unique notes from the whiskey. Oh, and definitely use sugar syrup instead of the solid stuff (or use a liquid substitute such as honey or maple syrup) – no one wants a grainy cocktail.

Method

Take a long zest of orange using a peeler and set aside. Place a big piece of ice in your rocks glass and put it all in the freezer. Fill a mixing glass with cubed ice and add the sugar, bitters and half the bourbon. Stir well (but not frantically). Add the second half of the bourbon and give a quick stir, strain over the block of ice in the rocks glass, and twist the orange peel over the top.

Magic

Endless possibilities! Old Fashioneds are exciting and you can have fun switching the sweetener, spirit, garnish or bitters. Any spirit works and as long as you follow the right balance you'll end up with a sophisticated cocktail that will showcase new sides to your favourite tipple. For example: tequila with honey, orange bitters, tabasco, grapefruit twist; blended scotch with peated malt, demerara sugar syrup, ginger bitters, banana slice; gin with pink peppercorn sugar syrup, Peychaud's bitters, lemon and orange zests…

MANHATTAN

Gather

1 orange

1 lemon

600ml/24oz rye whiskey

12 shots (300ml/12oz) sweet vermouth

1 shot (25ml/1oz) maraschino liqueur

½ teaspoon Peychaud's bitters

1 teaspoon Angostura bitters

Bottle

Small chilled cocktail glasses

Cubed ice

Cherry, to garnish (I like proper cocktail cherries like Luxardo or Fabbri, or fresh ones, but steer clear of the super-sweet candied type!)

It's hard to find an absolute *ultimate* of anything, but this has been my go-to drink for so many years that it could make a fair claim to the throne. Satisfying, rich and complex, it's peerless when I need something to settle body and soul late in the evening. I have several versions I'm keen on (all in the sweet camp, using rosso vermouth), but mixing it in batches like this makes it so easy to serve when you get home and just need a Manhattan – or if you have a group over for dinner.

Method

Cut 4 strips of orange zest and 1 strip of lemon zest using a peeler. Add the lemon zest and three strips of the orange to a large jug. Add the rye whiskey, vermouth, maraschino liqueur and bitters. Mix well. Rest for 10 minutes, strain, then bottle and chill.

To serve, add 2 shots (50ml/2oz) to a mixing glass filled with ice, then stir. Strain into a chilled cocktail glass, and garnish with a cherry and the remaining orange twist.

Magic

This serve is perfectly balanced and has enough alcohol in it to sit happily in your fridge for a while. You can change the ratios of liquids to equal parts for a softer version (and brands, bitters, additions etc), or invert the rye and vermouth quantities to give a vermouth-heavy Reverse Manhattan: it's gentler, for when you need a midweek reviver that doesn't pack too powerful a punch.

BROOKLYN

Gather

1½ shots (40ml/1.5oz) bourbon

1 tablespoon sweet vermouth

1 tablespoon Amer Picon

1 teaspoon maraschino liqueur

2 dashes orange bitters

Small, chilled cocktail glass

Cubed ice

Orange, to garnish

When you need that extra touch of luxury, the Brooklyn really fits the bill. It's a very close cousin of a Manhattan, but the additional bitterness has such a pleasing presence that this drink deserves its own spot. It uses Amer Picon – a tart liqueur that's often paired with beer in France. If you can't find it, an Italian amaro works a treat too. It's a classic post-dinner cocktail, but you'd be surprised by how well it goes with a nice rich dessert. And if you've just had one of those days, a Brooklyn will be there to help you get over it!

Method

Add all the ingredients to a mixing glass filled with ice and stir for about 20 seconds. Cut a swathe of orange peel using a peeler. Strain into a small, chilled cocktail glass and garnish with the orange twist.

Magic

The Brooklyn's bitter-orange depth makes it an intriguing variant of the classic Manhattan, but other flavours can work too. The recipe above hinges on a touch of bittersweetness, but other liqueurs such as Cointreau or green chartreuse instead of maraschino are worth a try, or even something similarly weighty such as coffee liqueur.

SMOKED WATERMELON SHANDY

150g/6oz diced watermelon
(frozen works perfectly if fresh is
not available)

1 teaspoon peated scotch (Lagavulin
works best)

2 teaspoons sugar syrup

1 tablespoon lime juice

1 chilli slice (optional)

300ml/12oz tropical-style IPA

Chilled small highball

Cubed ice

Flaked sea salt, to garnish

Nutribullet or blender

There's something lovely about a drink that is designed for two – of course it's great to be able to scale up when you've got a bigger group – but having a drink that suits sharing with someone dear is where cocktails really become super magical. With that in mind, I've turned to partner in Lyan (and various other) crimes, brother and dear pal Alex Lawrence Milia. He's created something that's ideal as a Friday party starter, or something that's great to catch up over – with or without food.

Method

Add the watermelon, scotch, sugar syrup, lime juice, chilli (if using) and 4 ice cubes to a nutribullet or similar high-speed blender and blend until smooth.

Add to a chilled highball rimmed with salt and slowly top with the IPA.

Magic

Fruits, whiskies and beers vary hugely, so as always, check the sweetness, heat or smokiness and flavour style to find your perfect match, but also switch up the profile using different brands – the key is to have something that feels layered and bright the way a great frozen drink should! Many modern IPAs have a tropical lean courtesy of New World hops, and suitably match wonderfully with the watermelon and the smoke, but you can also contrast using a more citrus-style beer.

RAMBLES

It's amazing how much better
a dram tastes outdoors. It warms
chilled limbs and fortifies in just
the right way. You need a cocktail
that heats from the inside - a
reward on a cold wander or long
walk with friends.

SMOKED SBITEN

Gather

5g/0.2oz loose-leaf
lapsang souchong tea

300ml/12oz water

4 shots (100ml/4oz) honey

10 shots (250ml/10oz)
fruitier style red wine

10 shots (250ml/10oz) blackberry jam

1 chilli slice

1 cinnamon stick, halved

2 cloves

1 thumb unpeeled ginger, sliced

¼ fresh nutmeg

4 shots (100ml/4oz) VSOP cognac

Flask and cups

Foraged pine, to garnish

There are lots of flavours in this drink that are reminiscent of being in nature to me, and taste better in the cool outdoors. There are also hints of the scents you find on a walk – the hedgerow aromas via blackberries, the hint of chimney smoke found in the leather and fruitiness of cognac, and the mix of florals and forest floor notes of a great honey. I've also nodded to all this nostalgia with some pine as the garnish. It was something we've used lots of in the bars, and the fruity, green (and obviously pine-y) aromas are an amazing ingredient that you can find all over the world. Sbiten is a warming drink I discovered on my travels in Russia, and has a wonderful balance of the tea tannins, fruit sweetness and spice. I've had it in both alcoholic and boozeless styles but this ratio plays to the best balance of each element for me.

Method

Brew the lapsang souchong by adding the loose-leaf tea to the water in a pot and cooking at 90°C/200°F for 2 minutes, then strain.

Add the tea, honey, wine, jam, chilli, cinnamon, cloves, ginger and nutmeg to a pan. Bring to the boil and stir for 2 minutes, then allow to cool. Pass through a sieve.

Add the cognac to the flask, then heat the strained Sbiten base mixture until just below the boil, and decant into the thermos. Serve in cups along your walk, ideally garnished with some fresh pine (cleaned, and ensured it's not yew) foraged from your rambles.

Magic

You can vary the spices, and the booze easily here – it's also great as a boozeless drink with the same warming, restorative qualities – and of course the quality of your ingredients changes the profile hugely. The real stars of the show are the honey, tea and jam – a forest honey and a local jam will always carry the complexity of brambles better, and a raw sprig of pine is the perfect garnish. Also, try to get a loose-leaf tea that isn't just laden with smoke, but has a green ethereal note to it if possible.

HUNTER'S FLASK

Gather

1 conference or williams pear

1 thumb ginger

4 shots (100ml/4oz) gin

8 shots (200ml/8oz) sweet-style whisky
(a lighter Speyside or an Irish whiskey
are ideal)

1 punnet blackberries

2 rosemary sprigs

50g/2oz demerara sugar

6 shots (150ml/6oz) water

Hip flask

This is my ideal companion on a long country ramble. It's a simple infusion but it captures and preserves the best of its fruits and herbs. And it simply needs bottling in a flask and drinking at body temperature. The rosemary and ginger provide a brilliant glow, and although gin and whisky might not seem like natural bedfellows, their sweet malt and herbal notes balance really well. You can change up the fruits according to your mood or what's available but I tend to combine a fruit, herb and a spice. Just remember to go with warming flavours.

Method

Chop the pear and the ginger and put into a medium-sized jar together with the blackberries. Mix the gin and whisky, and add to the jar. Leave to infuse overnight.

The next day, remove the fruit from the jar with a slotted spoon and add it to a pan. Add the rosemary, sugar and water and bring to the boil. Remove from the heat. Mix with the infused gin/whisky blend and allow to cool. Pass through a sieve and pour into a hip flask.

Magic

Nothing pairs better with this cocktail than freshly picked brambles – remember this if you stumble across them while strolling! A friend and I once missed a train while sipping a Hunter's Flask and devouring a stash of particularly sweet berries from a wild bush.

APPLE THREE WAYS

Gather

1 cardamom pod

300ml/12oz cider brandy
(Somerset cider brandy, bonded
applejack or calvados)

4 shots (100ml/4oz) gin

2 sliced apples (or 4 small ones)

1 litre/40oz cloudy apple juice

8 shots (200ml/8oz) unfiltered
cider vinegar

8 shots (200ml/8oz) honey

Pinch of salt and pepper

Pre-warmed insulated flask

A hot punch is easy to carry around in a flask and this recipe is splendid for when you need something to keep you toasty. It can be kept warm at home to welcome people returning out of the cold, but what you really want is a good occasion to be outdoors to enjoy it in its ideal setting.

Method

Gently squeeze the cardamom pod and drop into a pot. Add the other ingredients and warm over a gentle heat until it begins to steam. Stir to dissolve the honey, then fish out the cardamom. Pour into the flask.

Magic

Baking the apples beforehand with a little unrefined sugar creates an amazing depth in this drink. Simply scoop out most of the core with a melon-baller, fill with sugar and pop in the oven until soft. A traditional hot punch known as 'Wassail' often also contained eggs, although it doesn't travel well (eggs and flasks aren't buddies). But if you want to try the richer version, whisk two eggs, and slowly fold them through the heated punch mix.

CHILLED SMOKE AND MELONS

Gather

8 shots (200ml/8oz) peated scotch
(clean and light, such as Kilchoman,
Ardmore or Caol Ila)

4 shots (100ml/4oz) water

4 shots (100ml/4oz) Merlet
crème de melon

4 shots (100ml/4oz) Cocchi Americano

2 shots (50ml/2oz) fino sherry

Bottle

Rocks glasses

Rosemary sprig, to garnish

A faint whisper of smoke makes this outdoor drink curiously soothing.
It's not served hot, but you don't need a fridge – just allow the bottle
to cool in a gently running stream (or out in the cold!), then serve with
freshly plucked rosemary, a few gorse flowers or another (edible!) wild
herb. Although peated whiskies might seem a bit assertive when smelled
neat, they hide a multitude of wonderful fruit and spice notes that reveal
themselves when the malt is mixed. I do love the fruits concealed in big,
powerful whiskies such as Lagavulin and Talisker, but in this cocktail a
meeker variety is better suited.

Method

Mix all the ingredients and bottle.
Pour into glasses and garnish with a
rosemary sprig.

Magic

A restrained, elegant melon flavour can
be hard to achieve. The freshness of the
Merlet liqueur is great, but if you can't
get a hold of that, infuse some sliced
cantaloupe or honeydew melon into the
mix along with some sugar, rest for an
hour, then strain.

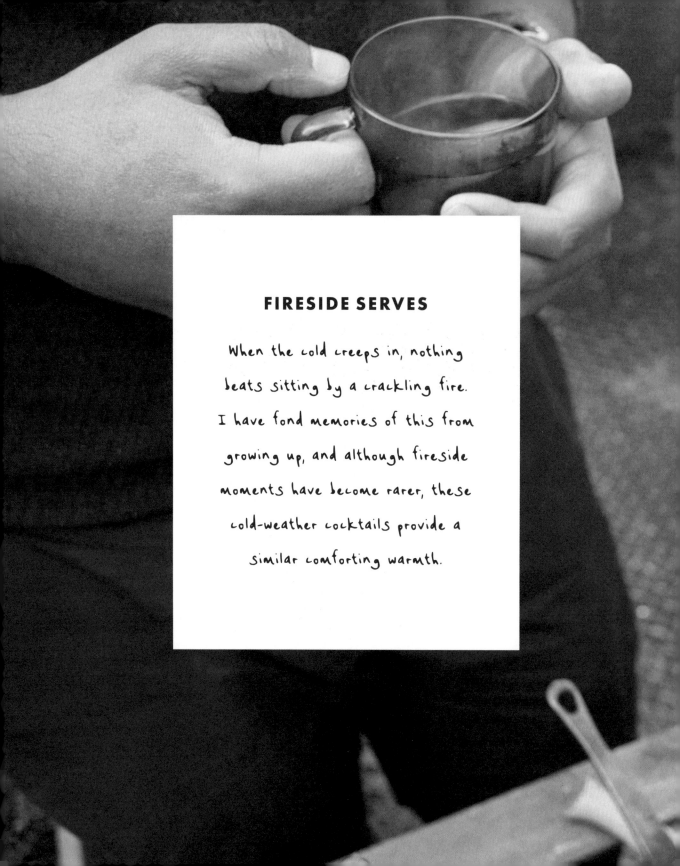

FIRESIDE SERVES

When the cold creeps in, nothing beats sitting by a crackling fire. I have fond memories of this from growing up, and although fireside moments have become rarer, these cold-weather cocktails provide a similar comforting warmth.

HOT COLD TEA

Gather

10g/0.4oz rooibos tea

300ml/12oz cold water

2 teaspoons maple syrup

Pinch flaked sea salt

Just over a shot (30ml/1.2oz)
blanco tequila

2 teaspoons Talisker 10 year old scotch

1 gelatin sheet

100g/4oz egg whites

100g/4oz white sugar

Highball

Soda siphon

N₂O charger

Cubed ice

This was inspired by a serve given to me by my dear friend Henrietta of Rare Tea Company and some of the experiments I did with her rooibos tea. The tea is wonderfully complex, with notes of honey as well as a lovely broken branch aroma that's simultaneously nutty and green. Try to seek out her version as it's a wonderful example of this wild crop, but just use the best you can find and use a loose-leaf tea if possible. The foam is slightly fiddly, but all you need is a soda siphon and some N₂O chargers (nitrous). The contrast of a warm foam with a cold drink is a lovely balance for the colder months.

Method

Cold brew the tea by adding the rooibos to the water and infusing in the fridge for 24 hours. Strain, then add the maple syrup, salt, tequila and scotch. Stir to ensure it is all incorporated, then chill well.

Bloom the gelatin in a bowl of cold water. Whisk together the egg whites and sugar in a separate bowl. Once mixed, squeeze out the gelatin and whisk it into the sugar-egg white mix. Pour this into your siphon, and add the container to a simmering pot of water for at least 30 minutes to warm through. Shake periodically, then charge with the N₂O charger and keep warm in the water.

To serve, pour your cold mixture over ice in the highball, then carefully decant the hot foam over the top.

Magic

You can easily flavour the foam by adding an accent to the sugar content, or by spritzing citrus oils over the top. A soda siphon is a very versatile tool, and although having to buy an extra piece of equipment might seem a faff, they're very useful items – you can also rapidly infuse spirits with herbs and spices by adding all to the canister, charging, shaking for a couple of minutes, then venting the gas and filtering.

BRANDY BLAZER

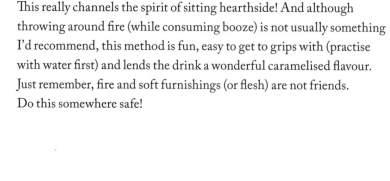

This really channels the spirit of sitting hearthside! And although throwing around fire (while consuming booze) is not usually something I'd recommend, this method is fun, easy to get to grips with (practise with water first) and lends the drink a wonderful caramelised flavour. Just remember, fire and soft furnishings (or flesh) are not friends. Do this somewhere safe!

Gather

Boiling water

1 teaspoon demerara sugar

2 shots (50ml/2oz) cognac

1 shot (25ml/1oz) crème de mûre

2 dashes Angostura bitters

Pre-warmed cup

Orange, to garnish

Method

Warm two pans on the hob by filling with boiling water from the kettle, allow to simmer, then tip out. Also pre-heat your cup with boiling water, but don't put that on the hob.

Using a peeler, remove a strip of orange peel.

Add 4 shots/100ml/4oz of boiling water and sugar to one of the pans, and the booze and bitters to the other.

Using a taper or long match, set the now-warm alcohol aflame and pour in an arc into the pan containing the boiling water. Repeat the process, pouring back and forth between the two pans – carefully. You should see and hear a stream of blue flame flowing. Extinguish by clapping the base of one of the pans on top of the other, then pour into your pre-warmed cup and garnish with the orange twist.

Magic

You can play with lots of flavours here: any spirit with a little sugar (and a high enough alcohol content) will be excellent, as the fire teases out rich notes. I love the herbiness that a touch of chartreuse brings: the flames won't burn off too much of its alcohol, so it remains fairly potent, but the added caramelisation and aeration from the fire-throwing gives a unique spice.

HOT BUTTERED GIN

Gather

Gather

4 shots (100ml/4oz) cider

Just over 1 shot (30ml/1.2oz) 10-year-old cider brandy (or bonded applejack or calvados)

1 tablespoon gin

1 tablespoon honey

2 teaspoons lemon juice

Pre-warmed teacup

Lemon, to garnish

Small slice of butter, to garnish

Hot Buttered Rum is an esteemed and ancient cockle-warmer that teams spice with the richness of melting butter. Here I've switched to a lighter version, dispensing with the grog and bringing in gin, cider brandy and hard cider to lift the drink. Using butter might seem weird, but it supplies a truly lovely savoury edge.

Method

Place the cider in a pan and gently warm up.

Add the cider brandy, gin, honey and lemon juice to your cup. Mix, then top with the hot cider. Cut off a twist of lemon peel and add it, then drop in a pad of butter.

Magic

To make a simple flavoured butter, allow it to soften slightly, then fold spices, finely sliced herbs or citrus in, then chill to set again. The infusions will end up in your mug as the butter melts, of course, so stick with less 'bitty' spices.

BUMPED HOT CHOCOLATE

Gather

1 tablespoon chartreuse

1 tablespoon poire william

1 teaspoon unrefined sugar

4 shots (100ml/4oz) whole milk

Pinch vanilla salt (a vanilla pod split
and infused into sea salt for at least a day)

30g/1oz good dark chocolate

Pre-warmed mug

Nutmeg or cinnamon, to finish

Proper, thick hot chocolate is rich and soothing (I first had it in New York, then became obsessed with it in Spain), and I love having it like this, with mild herbal and fruity touches. I prefer to use real chocolate and unhomogenised, local milk, as it brings a luxurious intensity, but use drinking chocolate if you prefer.

Method

Pour the chartreuse and poire william into a pre-warmed mug.

Add the sugar, milk, vanilla salt and chocolate to a pot and heat. Whisk constantly but don't allow to boil. When gently steaming, pour over the liqueurs in your mug and top with some freshly grated nutmeg or cinnamon.

Magic

You can make this very condensed by using cream (as well as milk) with extra chocolate and serving much shorter. You can also layer in extra flavours by warming spices in the milk then straining them off – anise, basil, chilli and fruits all can be incorporated successfully into chocolate – and changing the liqueurs to match your tastes is a fine idea too.

HET PINT

Gather

2 organic eggs

Pinch vanilla salt
(see Bumped Hot Chocolate, p181)

300ml/12oz golden ale
(something sweet, rather than too
hoppy. A dark beer will work too)

4 shots (100ml/4oz) scotch

3 tablespoons demerara sugar

Pre-warmed mugs

Nutmeg, to finish

Hot beer and eggs is definitely not your everyday sort of cocktail partnership, but bear with me here. This old recipe was introduced to me by my dear friend, esteemed mentor and partner in whisky-based crimes Dave Broom – and I always turn to it for a luxurious and reassuring treat. Use the best eggs you can and it won't taste at all eggy – it will simply have a luscious texture and weight. This recipe makes a decent-sized batch, and even a little bit is greatly soothing, so it should serve a few people.

Method

Crack your eggs into a pan and whisk with the salt.

Add the ale, whisky and sugar to another pot and heat until steaming (don't boil). Whisk to dissolve the sugar and remove from the heat. Pour into the egg mix while whisking constantly. Pour into the mugs and finish with some freshly grated nutmeg.

Magic

The beer you use will change the weight and feel of the drink enormously. Another favourite version of mine is to use stout and a few raspberries thrown into the mix.

FIRESIDE FLIP

Gather

1 coin of ginger

1 tablespoon honey

Just over 1 shot (30ml/1.2oz) sloe gin

1 shot (25ml/1oz) honeyed-style malt whisky (such as Highland Park 12 year old, or Aberfeldy 12 year old)

1 whole egg

Dash Angostura bitters

Chilled sherry glass

Cubed ice

Nutmeg, to finish

Flips are an old family of drinks that use whole eggs to marvellous effect. In some ways these drinks are basically boozy custard, which tastes every bit as delicious as you'd expect it would be. This Fireside Flip has comforting, malty notes matched with the fruity/nutty flavours of sloe gin, all tied up together neatly with a hint of golden spice from honey and ginger. It's at its best made two-in-a-shaker for you and a loved one (just double the ingredients in this recipe).

Method

Crush the ginger and honey in the shaker. Add the other ingredients and shake without ice, then shake with ice and double strain into your glass (see p27). Garnish with fresh nutmeg.

Magic

Using a ginger jam or marmalade in place of the fresh ginger tempers some of its mild heat and draws forth a slightly more 'golden' taste. You could try gently cooking down the ginger in the honey to tame some of its citric spice: this also adds an appealing new dimension to the drink.

WINTER FEASTING

Cold weather outdoors is a
fine excuse for getting together
indoors. It's often nicer to stay
in, and the chill makes warming
flavours taste even more appealing.
These drinks celebrate this (and are
blissfully easy to make).

BARLEY CHAMPAGNE

A favourite hosting approach for me has always been to bottle up a base, then top up with bubbles as guests arrive. It works wonderfully during other seasons too, but I find that particularly around the festive periods, when people are much more lax with timings, having something that can be poured quickly at the last minute, to get everyone a drink without taking you away from the celebrations, is a great plan. This might seem very bright in profile, but it works perfectly with any true dry sparkling wine to accentuate the characteristics – but you can easily go big and powerful with flavours, too!

Gather

4 shots (100ml/4oz) water

6 shots (150ml/6oz) lemon barley water cordial

8 shots (200ml/8oz) fino sherry or dry vermouth

12 shots (300ml/12oz) London dry gin

10 dashes Tabasco

Bottle

Chilled flutes

Chilled champagne or traditional method sparkling wine, to finish

Rosemary sprigs, to garnish

Method

Add the water, cordial, sherry or vermouth and gin to a jug, then add the Tabasco. Stir and then decant into the clean wine bottle and chill well.

To serve, add a shot and a half (40ml/1.5oz) of the chilled mixture to a flute, then top with bubbles. Add a sprig of rosemary and serve.

Magic

You can make lemon barley cordial at home (it's a very old-fashioned British cordial of pearl barley and lemon) but this recipe works great with any store-bought cordial that brings sweetness and acidity. Elderflower, blackcurrant or even more regional ones such as redcurrant or gooseberry also work – although there's a richness to the barley addition that works wonderfully. Tabasco adds a background heat, but try adding other accent spices such as gochujang or sriracha – just sieve it after mixing to remove any particulates as they will interfere with the fizz. Plus you just want a hint of fruity warmth, else you'll throw the balance of the drink!

GALLE HOUSE PUNCH

Gather

1 teaspoon black peppercorns

2 cardamom pods

1 stick cinnamon

½ nutmeg

1 thumb ginger

6 cloves

500g/20oz sugar

250ml/10oz water

1 flowering tea bud

300ml/12oz boiling water

8 shots (200ml/8oz) golden rum

4 shots (100ml/4oz) dark rum

6 shots (150ml/6oz) lemon juice

6 shots (150ml/6oz) cloudy apple juice

500ml/20oz dry cider (hard cider!)

Punch bowl and cups

Fire poker or similar

Spiced bread or cake to finish

This punch is named for our old family house in Sri Lanka and uses many of the spices that were grown there. It's a dramatically warming cocktail, so I suggest warming it in a suitably dramatic style! Using a loggerhead (a poker warmed in the embers of a fire, bonfire or on the hob) is a great party trick – and not only does it heat up the punch, it lends a lovely caramelised note and an essence of wood smoke. If you don't have a poker, you can of course brew the tea, warm the ingredients on the hob, and then mix the two.

Method

Nestle the poker in the embers of a fire (or in a bonfire or on the hob).

To make a spiced syrup, bash the peppercorns, cardamom, cinnamon, nutmeg, ginger and cloves in a pestle and mortar. Add the water to a pot and heat. When boiling, add the sugar and ground spices, then remove from the heat. Stir, allow to cool, then strain through a sieve.

Place the tea bud in the punch bowl, add the boiling water and allow to steep for 1 minute. Add the remaining ingredients plus 4 shots (100ml/4oz) of your spiced syrup. Remove the now red-hot poker from the fire and slowly plunge into the punch. When it stops fizzing, remove and ladle the punch into cups. Dunk bread in for extra tastiness.

Magic

Vary the spices according to the tea, cider and rums you're planning to use. As well as the aromatic varieties above, cumin, fennel, citrus peel and the like can all bring something to the party too. And – butter the bread!

NUKED NEGRONI

Gather

1 grapefruit

12 shots (300ml/12oz) gin

12 shots (300ml/12oz) sweet vermouth

12 shots (300ml/12oz) Campari

6 blackberries

1 rosemary sprig

Bottle

Rocks glass

Big ice cubes

This is a simple and quick infusion I like to do. It pulls together some incredible bittersweet flavours which really complement the much-loved classic Negroni. It's an amazing cocktail to have to hand: simply grab from the fridge, pour over ice and garnish. The blackberry coaxes some of the fruit out of the Campari and vermouth, while the rosemary delivers a welcome herbal dryness. Microwaves can be terrible for food, but really useful for drinks!

Method

Take a strip of zest from the grapefruit using a peeler and add to a microwave-safe bowl with the other ingredients. Cover, then blast in a microwave for 3 minutes on full power. Allow to cool, then strain and bottle.

To serve, fill a rocks glass with ice, pour a healthy measure and garnish with a slice of grapefruit.

Magic

Using a microwave is an effortless way to infuse. Making a Negroni like this is a pretty bulletproof method, but to mix things up you could vary the proportions of spirits. You could also try replacing some or all of the elements (for example, take out half the Campari and sub in Aperol or another bitters), and have fun changing the fruits and herbs. Overdilution will kill the drink though, so try and keep the mix cold by using big bits of ice and a chilled glass.

BLA BLA FIX

Gather

300ml/12oz blueberry juice

350g/14oz sugar

½ teaspoon yellow pectin

2 teaspoons honey

2 shots aquavit

Just under 1 shot (20ml/0.8oz) lemon juice

1 teaspoon crème de cassis, or blackcurrant cordial

Cocktail glass

Cubed ice

I began drinking aquavit – a strongly herbal spirit – when visiting my friend Nick in Sweden and after I met my dear Norwegian buddy Anette. This local speciality goes perfectly chilled alongside a mountain of crayfish (if you're not lucky enough to live somewhere that prizes these crustaceans, befriend a Norwegian/Dane/Swede just for this midsummer feast) and also comes with a herbaceous edge quite distinct from gin. The blueberry paint here is a trick borrowed from my bar White Lyan. It sits on the rim of the glass allowing a teasing sweetness before the sourness from the drink washes over. You could just add blueberry to the drink, but it creates a very different effect (and doesn't look nearly as good).

Method

To make the paint, add the blueberry, sugar and pectin to a pot and heat on a low/medium heat, stirring regularly, for 30 minutes. Allow to cool.

Take a cocktail glass, dip a brush in paint (removing the excess), then confidently swipe around the inside of the rim. Place the glass into a freezer to chill while you assemble the drink.

Add the honey, aquavit, lemon and blackcurrant (liqueur or cordial) to a shaker. Stir to dissolve the honey, shake with cubed ice. Double strain into chilled, painted glass (see p27). Then sip away!

Magic

You can make a paint with other juices, but it's best to use something with a nice sweet/sour balance: think pomegranate, cherry or the like. If you can't get pectin, use jam sugar (which contains pectin), or throw in a couple of lemon pips.

BREWED BROOKLYN

Gather

1 orange

4 shots (100ml/4oz) india pale ale

4 shots (100ml/4oz) stout

2 shots (50ml/2oz) amaro

8 shots (200ml/8oz) water

500ml/20oz rye whiskey

8 raspberries

Pinch fennel seeds

Pinch dried wormwood

½ teaspoon dandelion root

½ teaspoon burdock root

100g/4oz sugar

Bottle

Chilled cocktail glasses

So good it appears twice! This is a variant on a variant of my aforementioned favourite cocktail, the Manhattan (see p153 and p154). Its bitter kick turns it into a more characterful version, and making it like this in a batch means you can keep it chilled ahead of a group of friends coming round. It doesn't feel quite at home in the early evening, though: this one really comes to life after dark!

Method

Cut the zest off the orange and add it to a microwave-safe bowl. Then add all the remaining ingredients to the bowl. Whisk to remove some of the froth from the beer and dissolve the sugar.

When settled, cover and heat in a microwave for 3 minutes on full power.

Allow to cool and strain (try to use a fine sieve or muslin if possible as the wormwood is pretty fine). Store in a bottle. Chill well, then serve.

Magic

The microwave gives an intense exposure to heat which cuts out as soon as the timer elapses, but don't heat so much the mix evaporates. This way the whole will concentrate in on itself giving the richness you're after. That said, you might have to vary proportions a bit dependent on the ingredients you have. Play around with complementing the booze through your botanicals too.

SPICED CRANBERRIES WITH CHAMPAGNE

Gather

1 orange

3 tablespoons fresh cranberries

4 shots (100ml/4oz) cranberry juice

1 star anise

3 cloves

100g/4oz sugar

1 tablespoon curaçao

1 tablespoon cognac

Flutes

Cubed ice

Chilled champagne, to finish

A bit of fizz always goes down well in a gathering, and when fresh cranberries start to appear as the months get colder, I find combining the two a much more agreeable option than making boring old sauce. The berries are nicely tart, so marrying them with the vitality of the champagne and some sweetness draws out the best in them. They make a great garnish to the drink too!

Method

Zest the orange using a peeler, then juice it, straining off any seeds or bits of pulp.

To make cranberry syrup, add the cranberries, orange and cranberry juices, anise, clove and peel to a small pot along with the sugar and warm gently. Stir to dissolve the sugar then remove from the heat. When cool, fish out the spices and peel but leave the cranberries in.

Put the cognac and curaçao in a mixing glass filled with ice. Add 1 tablespoon of the cranberry syrup and stir. Strain into a flute, add one or two cranberries from the syrup and top with champagne.

Magic

Gently poaching the cranberries will mean they keep a lot of their lovely sharpness. But if you want them a little sweeter, cook the cranberries down for a few minutes and they'll soften and sweeten.

BOTTLED SWEET MARTINI

Gather

8 shots (200ml/8oz) gin

6 shots (150ml/6oz) apple brandy
(Somerset cider brandy, bonded
applejack or calvados)

6 shots (150ml/6oz) sweet vermouth

2 shots (50ml/2oz) apricot liqueur
(such as Merlet)

8 dashes orange bitters

4 shots (100ml/4oz) mineral water

Bottle

Chilled cocktail glasses

Lemon, to garnish

Sweet martinis are a rare choice nowadays, but their mouth-filling lusciousness becomes much more appealing when it's cold outside. Somewhere between an Angel Face (gin, apple brandy and apricot) and a Sweet Martini (gin and sweet vermouth), this is a great version to bottle up and have ready in the fridge for when you need a cocktail at a minute's notice. It'll last, so there's no worry about it going off, but I find most people can't get enough and the batch goes in one sitting. Pre-diluting means you don't need any equipment on the spot, and saves a huge amount of hassle if you've got thirsty friends!

Method

Mix all ingredients in a large jug. Bottle, then chill well. Cut a small coin of lemon peel. Pour a measure from the bottle into the chilled glasses. Snap the coin of lemon over the top and drop in.

Magic

This cocktail is a satisfying balance of dry, rich and sweet. It dances around your palate rather merrily, but if you prefer it slightly sweeter still, bump the gin and apple brandy to 6 measures each, and mix with 3 shots each of vermouth and apricot.

NY SNAP

Gather

Just over 1 shot (30ml/1.2oz) cognac

2 teaspoons golden rum

1 clove

2 shots (50ml/2oz) pineapple juice

1 tablespoon sugar syrup (see p31)

2 teaspoons lemon juice

2 teaspoons red wine (claret, aka
Bordeaux, is ideal)

2 dashes Angostura bitters

Flute

Cubed ice

Although this cocktail is served cold, the flavours have a lovely cosying-up effect. It borrows from the claret 'snap' in a New York Sour (a whiskey sour with a small float of red wine over the surface) to give a little warmth and some drying tannins. It's one to share between you and just one other lucky person – two serves will fit a shaker snugly (just double the ingredients in this recipe).

Method

Shake all ingredients with ice except the wine and bitters, and double strain into a flute (see p27). Mix the wine and bitters in a small jug and pour slowly over the back of a teaspoon to float on top of the drink.

Magic

The float imparts an amazing aroma, and gently imbues each sip with a little taste of the wine. With this in mind, you can layer in some extra flavour (nutmeg works brilliantly), or substitute some or all of the wine – a splash of port or apricot brandy is amazing here.

BELLE BALL

This is a drink I've made for my wife Annabelle when we've needed a winter warmer, or when the season has caught up on us and we need a little reviver ahead of an evening out! The base spiced tea is great as a restorative, but using the whiskey profile that is packed with botanical flavours, and some elderberry richness, makes it perfect when you need a hug coming in from the cold. The whiskey does all the heavy lifting here.

Gather

1 teaspoon coriander seeds

½ teaspoon black peppercorns

1 clove

1 cardamom pod

300ml/12oz water

½ thumb unpeeled ginger, sliced

Just over a shot (30ml/1.2oz)
Fierfield Barberry whiskey

Just under a shot (20ml/0.8oz)
lemon juice

1 heaped teaspoon melipona or
wildflower honey

Ceramic mug

Wheel of lemon, to garnish

Method

Lightly toast the coriander seeds, peppercorns, clove and cardamom in a pot, then add the water and ginger and bring to the boil. Simmer for 2 minutes, then remove from the heat.

Add the whiskey, lemon juice and honey to a mug and stir. Strain the botanical tea over the top, stir, then garnish with the lemon wheel.

Magic

Fierfield Barberry is something I made with my dear friend Louise from JJ Corry to celebrate the history of farm whiskey infusions, and to embrace the amazing producers around Ireland. The Barberry edition is rich and autumnal and adds a wealth of complexity. If you can't find it, split the base with equal parts Irish single malt and some port.

SIMPLE SERVES

There's something uniquely restorative about gin and tonic, or a clean highball, but despite their apparent simplicity, they're often made terribly. Essentials are lots of ice (seriously, as much as you can fit in the glass!) and a crisp, very cold mixer - but a few twists up your sleeve make all the difference.

HOUSE G&T

This is one of the best versions of a gin and tonic, and my standard go-to when at home. Keep this template in mind when making yours – you can change all the additions, but the structure should remain. Keep everything cold if you can: gin and glassware in the freezer along with a tray full of good ice, and some small bottles of fresh tonic along with garnishes in the fridge. This will lead to an incredible experience (as long as you have the best ingredients you can get your hands on, and plenty of ice).

Gather

2 shots (50ml/2oz) frozen gin

Really cold tonic water

Small highball

Cubed ice

Lemon, to garnish

Large mint sprig, to garnish

Method

Using a peeler, cut two strips of lemon peel.

Fill your highball with ice, add the gin and slowly top with chilled tonic water. Stir gently then add a straw. Twist one of the lemon peels over the top then throw away. Give the mint a slap and tuck in alongside a straw. Twist the second lemon peel over the top and place alongside the mint.

Magic

This is a super-fresh style, as that's usually what I seek when I fancy a G&T, but you can play up to the botanicals in your chosen gin. The mint works sensationally, but add in other types of citrus zest and see how they lift the notes in the spirit, and how they lift your own spirits!

TIKI G&T

Gather

1 thick slice of watermelon

2 shots (50ml/2oz) frozen gin

Chilled tonic water

Small highball

Lemon, to garnish

A little fanciness every now and again is great (as long as it's not pompous), and this simple version of a G&T is every bit ab fab, channelling the over-the-top extravagant fun of tiki-style serves. Bringing a couple of these out to friends just looks amazing, and the contrast of the pink watermelon with the clear drink is a lovely take on the classic.

Method

Remove the peel of the watermelon and cut thick rods to fit the length and width of your glassware (not too snugly or else you'll end up with too strong a drink). Freeze them for at least two hours.

Cut a strip of lemon zest using a peeler. Place the frozen melon in your glass, add the cold gin and slowly top with tonic. Stir gently to mix then twist the lemon peel over the top.

Magic

The watermelon will go a little furry as it thaws, which isn't usually a problem, but to avoid you can compress the rods by placing in a bag and sucking all the air out using a vacuum sealer (if you happen to have one in your kitchen!). You can also juice the melon and freeze the strained juice in strips in an ice mould. Both will intensify the flavour a touch and help the texture as the drink mellows.

FANCY G&T

Pink gin (a simple mix of gin and Angostura bitters) is a fine, aromatic pre-dinner serve, but it can be a little intense. Paired with a zesty homemade sherbet and a herbal tonic, this version is awesome as an aperitif or end-of-day wonder.

Gather

2 grapefruits

100g/4oz sugar

2 dashes Angostura bitters

2 shots (50ml/2oz) frozen gin

Small highball

Cubed ice

Chilled Fever-Tree Mediterranean tonic water, to finish

Lemon, to garnish

Method

First up make the sherbet. Peel two grapefruits and add the peel to a bowl with the sugar. Grind the peel and sugar using the end of a rolling pin and leave to infuse for a couple of hours. After this, juice the grapefruits and add to the mix. Stir until all the sugar is dissolved, then strain.

Cut a strip of lemon using a peeler. Fill a highball with ice. Add the bitters, then the gin and just under 1 shot (20ml/0.8oz) of the sherbet. Stir well, add more ice, then top slowly with tonic and stir again. Twist the lemon peel over the top then place alongside a straw.

Magic

The sugar draws out all of the oils from the grapefruit peel to give the necessary sherbety tang. You can help this process along a bit by placing the sugar and peels in a bag and compressing using a vacuum sealer, if you have one. However, simply leaving the peels and sugar covered in a bowl for a few hours will give a similar effect.

JOLLY GREEN TONIC

Gather

Pinch sea salt

2 thyme sprigs or ½ teaspoon dried thyme

1 teaspoon soy lecithin powder

300ml/12oz boiling water

Cucumber

½ lime

2 shots (50ml/2oz) frozen gin

Small highball

Cubed ice

Chilled tonic water, to finish

The gin and tonic is a classic example of what we call a highball. Although the highball is ideal for an early-evening drink – and particularly the G&T, with its digestive qualities – it's also wonderful alongside food. This version employs a salted, herbal 'air' – a simple ultra-light foam that's great for transferring a wisp of a strong flavour. It's made using lecithin powder (easy to pick up at health food shops) and acts to trap air within the solution creating, essentially, an edible bubble bath.

Method

First, make the 'air'. Take a large bowl, and in it mix the salt, thyme, lecithin and boiling water, making sure all the powders dissolve. Tilt the bowl and place a stick blender near the surface. Mix on the high setting to force in lots of air. The lecithin will trap rising bubbles, forming the foam.

Using a peeler, cut a long strip of cucumber lengthwise (throw away the first few strips, which will just be skin).

Wrap the strip of cucumber around the inside of the glass then fill it with ice. Using a hand squeezer, juice the lime directly into the glass. Add the gin, stir gently, then top with tonic water. Add a straw. Skim off a scoop of the thyme air from your bowl and place on top of each glass.

Magic

A portable fish tank pump is a cheap and fun way to create the air. Put the air mixture in a small cup, then add the fish tank diffuser stone into the solution. As you switch it on, the pump will aerate the solution creating a mushroom of flavoured air – just remember to turn it off!

TEA & G

2 shots (50ml/2oz) frozen gin

½ teaspoon Earl Grey tea

Small highball

Cubed ice

Really cold tonic water, to finish

Wedge of grapefruit, to garnish

When it comes to a G&T, many of us think of the citrus notes of the gin, or the squeeze of lemon or lime over the top of the drink. They're uplifting and really what this cocktail is all about. Intensifying them is a great way of making it even more refreshing, but to balance it out, I use a touch of tannic bite from black tea. Go for a high-quality, loose-leaf tea that's scented with real bergamot. This supplies extra flavoursome citrus notes, rather than unpleasant bitter oils.

Method

Mix the frozen gin and the tea. Allow to stand for 1 minute, then strain. (This is usually the perfect time to cut a wedge of grapefruit and grab your ice – it's almost like it was meant to be.)

Add the infused gin to an ice-filled glass. Top with tonic and add a straw. Gently squeeze the grapefruit and add to the glass.

Magic

With the very best teas, the flavour changes with the number of infusions, so reserve the leaves to use again. I've been using Henrietta's Rare Tea Company teas for years - and the third infusion tends to be my favourite.

VERMOUTH & SODA

Gather

Just over 2 shots (60ml/2.4oz) dry vermouth such as Martini, Cocchi Americano or Dolin

4 shots (100ml/4oz) chilled soda water

Wine glass

Cubed ice

Slice fresh melon, to garnish

Lemon wheel, to garnish

Mint sprig, to garnish

I've spoken at length about the beauty of fortified wines, such as vermouths, and how using them in a variety of cocktails (or even dishes) is a great way of celebrating the delicacy of the wines. One way to really enjoy the range of flavours available is to make the wine the key component of a drink. There are so many styles available, from crisp, dry vermouths, floral biancos and nuttier amber styles through to a range of richer rossos or sweeter vermouths. Not to mention the fact you can match specific flavours to the wonderful (drier!) sodas now available – Noilly Prat with Fever-Tree's white grape and apricot is a total winner. To demonstrate the versatility, I'm suggesting a dry version that can easily be adapted with the ingredients you have available, but still manages to be a foolproof recipe that is suitable for most occasions.

Method

Fill a wine glass with ice, then add the vermouth, a slice of melon and a lemon wheel. Stir, then add more ice, then top with the soda water and garnish with a sprig of mint.

Magic

You can use this ratio with any vermouth – even the richer sweet styles work great lengthened with soda. The garnish has a similar versatility, with the melon contrasting the light bitterness, and the lemon playing alongside the herbal notes, but the mint is best suited to the greener notes of a dry or bianco vermouth. Once you start adding a bit of depth and colour, try using a herb that reflects the changes; basil works great.

WHITE PORT & TONIC

Gather

2 shots (50ml/2oz) white port

4 shots (100ml/4oz) chilled Fever-Tree tonic (or a good tonic without sweeteners)

Highball

Cubed ice

Citrus wheel, to garnish

Fresh herbs, to garnish

This is such a simple highball, and celebrates a product that many might have overlooked or not known what to do with. White port – the dry, crisp cousin of the more famous fortified wine – is, as the name suggests, white rather than ruby purple, and comes replete with zesty citrus notes and some of those wonderful green olive notes found in its cousin, fino sherry. It has a different acidity and nutty profile that makes it similarly wonderful, yet different in highball serves. The beauty of this is its versatility – keep everything cold, then choose a fruit and herb garnish to customise.

Method

Fill a highball with ice, then add the port. Stir, then add more ice, then top with tonic water and garnish with the citrus wheel and herbs.

Magic

Find the garnish combo that suits your palate and the side of the drink you want to pull out – pink grapefruit slice plus a basil leaf to show off the floral side, or lemon and thyme to pull out the greener notes. But any crisp fruit would work; try thin slices of apple, or even slices of tropical fruits. The drink might seem simple, but like the best cocktails, it has plenty of complexity and versatility.

INDEX

There are too many people to thank, always. But all this wouldn't be nearly as fun without the help of these folk.

Family

My dearest wife Annabelle (thank you for making me look at everything differently, and with so much more joy), Dragan, Natasha & Daniel & Jaya, Guy & Raven & Ember, Mamma, Dad and Kate, Marc, Pyper & Ashley, Karen-o, Iain (miss ya heaps brother), Alex & Maura (muchos kisses ya babes), Rob & Em, Vik & Laura & Leo, Bob & Gloria & kids, Batman, Barney, Rich, Jonny, Phil & Jo, Lizzie & Ben & kids, Antoine & Hannah & kids, Alex & Tanya & kids, Jenny, Edgar, Mirabelle & Ghislaine, Sarah & Ruby, Jam & Tash, Jonquil & Danny & kids, Mahi, Prathiba, Dumi & families, Yohan & Mandy, Alan & Gelareh, Elli, Bari, the Cheti, Dante, Chan and Jones and extended families, always.

Dearest friends

Teams Lyan – huge love to our big bosses Phoebe, James, Peter, John, Vlad, Stevie and all the teams at Mr Lyan Studio, Super Lyan, Silver Lyan, Seed Library and Lyaness, Robin & Jade, Nathan & Hana, Marcis, Team DL, Mayface, Zoë, Chris Stock, Jason Scott, Mike Aikman, Craig Harper, Ian McLaren, Stu McCluskey, Dr Johnny, Dr Arielle, Lewis Jaffrey, Tristan Stephenson, Dave Broom, Stu Bale, Family Boublil, Terri, Pauli, Niall & Lucy, Katie & Jezza, Shay, Neil & Joel, Dawn Davies, Mitch, Ben Slater, Todd Selby, Kiwi Nick, Henrietta & Rich, Griffiths family, Georgie Bell & Fab, Marco No Way, Dan Bartley, Kernohan & Neil & Alba, Greggy, Cindy Gallop.

Industry peeps

John, Chris & Compass Box, Gemma Bell, Kimberley Brown, Marco Pierre White, Liam Davy, Robin Gill, Beth Adams, Sam & Harry, Ali Burgess, Alex & Monica, Jim, Naren, Tina, Jonathan, Jason Cousins, James Lowe, Clove Club, Team Imbibe, Tien Ho, Joe & Jason, MRA-C, David Piper & Dunk, Marcin Miller, Ben Ellefson, Sukhinder & Raj, Eddy, Andy Gemmel, Darren & Nicole, Addie & Ally, Camille, Jo Lacey, Josh, JJ, Sean & Leanne, Jacob Briars, Derek Elefson, Tom Walker, Phil & Elayne, Sam & Michael, Paul Mant, John Gakuru, Cami & Hobby, Ross Purnell, Dan Gasper, Claire & Dan, Ras & Adi, Marius & Cask, Harold McGee, Dave Arnold, Ben Cleary, Master Paewai, Charles Spence, Rachel Dutton, Nick Morgan, Xabi & Edu, Team LX, Restaurant Noma, Lore, MasterClass and everyone who's loved and supported us.

The people that made it happen

Denise – thank you for encouraging this relook at something I have loved so much, Zena (I'm sorry. And my god you're patient. Thanks for believing in this), Kim Lightbody (this project has been so enjoyable to create; thanks for adding your magic), Eve O'Sullivan (for your amazing food), Glenn Howard, Euan Ferguson, Hilary Bird, John & Jay Jackson, Kevin Bacon, Jo & Ren, Lynn, Chris & babies, Charlie Hay, Elli, Baby & Gracie, Sylvia & Henry the beagle, Rosie, Charlotte, Daniel, Jackie, Joel, Kieran, Roselle, Eric & Emily, Michelle, Melissa & Brian, Batman.